I COULD HAVE KICKED MYSELF
DAVID FROST'S
BOOK OF THE WORLD'S WORST DECISIONS

Also Known As
The Hindsight Saga

I COULD HAVE KICKED MYSELF

Compiled and Written by
DAVID FROST and MICHAEL DEAKIN

Illustrated by
WILLIAM RUSHTON

ANDRE DEUTSCH

Research by
BARBARA TWIGG

First published 1982 by
André Deutsch Limited
105 Great Russell Street, London WC1

Copyright © 1982 by
David Paradine Productions Limited

Filmset by Pioneer
Printed in Great Britain by
Ebenezer Baylis & Son Limited
The Trinity Press, Worcester and London

ISBN 0 233 97419 9

ACKNOWLEDGEMENTS

The compilers would like to thank everyone whose brains they have inadvertently and, indeed, vertently picked during the preparation of this book. In particular the names of Norris McWhirter, General Sir John Hackett, Fenton Bresler, Arthur C. Clarke and H.S.H. Prince Rainier spring to mind.

From André Deutsch the contributions of Diana Athill, Piers Burnett and the Padrone were indispensable; and, as ever, the compilers could not have functioned at all without the efforts of Tricia Pombo and Cindy Ballin.

I COULD HAVE KICKED MYSELF
DAVID FROST'S
BOOK OF THE WORLD'S WORST DECISIONS

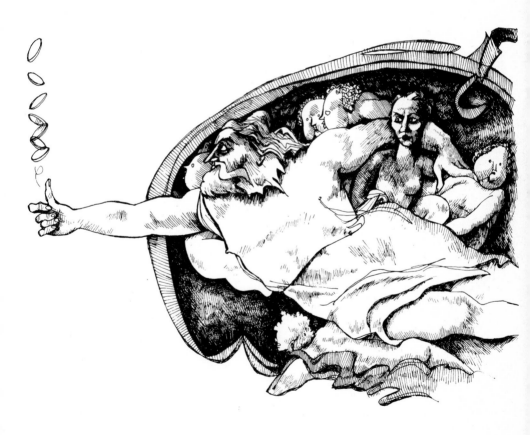

Introduction

The genesis of this book took place on a charter flight which Michael Deakin and I were making to Memphis, Tennessee, in the company of two hundred eager and worshipful Britishers. The object of their veneration was Elvis Presley and, entering into the spirit of the thing, the charter company had provided us with one of their most venerable planes. There were thus many hours, including a refuelling stop in Bangor, Maine, in which to read and re-read our piles of research. One particular story stood out.

Sam Phillips had been the owner of a minute downtown Memphis recording company, Sun Records. In 1955, in order to raise cash, Phillips had sold to RCA Records the exclusive contract he had with a young man with prominent sideburns who had wandered into his studio and cut a record on spec as a present for his mother. RCA paid Mr Phillips the not inconsiderable sum of $35,000, but even as he pocketed the cheque he was forfeiting all his royalties on more than a billion records — one for every four people on earth. Sam Phillips probably kicked himself many times in the years that followed.

Other incidents sprang to mind. I recalled an occasion which had involved a close friend, actress Janette Scott. She had been approached with an exhilarating offer — to play the lead on Broadway in a new musical called *My Fair Lady*. At the time, Janette was not a free agent. As a popular child star — at the time of the *My Fair Lady* offer she was still only fifteen — she was signed to a stern and unbending contract with the Associated British Picture Corporation which gave them a veto power over all her professional activities. Nevertheless, on this occasion, she and her mother Thora Hird had few doubts about obtaining the necessary go-ahead from C.J. Latta, then head of ABPC. Mr Latta listened to their excited account of this unique opportunity, paused for a moment and then uttered the immortal words, 'A musical of *Pygmalion*? Who on earth would want to go and see that? It could do your career immense damage — *no*.'

Janette had no reason to kick herself — she had done her best — and C.J. Latta probably never kicked himself either; but certainly, given the opportunity, Janette would have been less than human if she had not been sorely tempted to kick C.J. Latta! (Though in fairness to Mr Latta, it can be added that two other people rejected the concept of turning *Pygmalion* into a musical when it was first suggested to them, and they were Alan Jay Lerner and Frederick Loewe).

Since the trip that Michael and I were making was for an ITV documentary, *Elvis — He Touched Their Lives*, it was only natural that the talk of bad decisions turned to television, and Michael recalled Lord Beaverbrook's decision back in the early fifties not to take a proffered holding in ITV with the words, 'We are first and foremost newspaper men.'

He made that decision in order to preserve the character of the House of Beaverbrook as a predominantly newspaper empire but, for want of that very investment, the Beaverbrook era came to an end in 1978 and his beloved

10

Daily Express, with annual losses of £2 million, had to be sold to Trafalgar House.

Once launched on this conversation, we found other examples coming to mind. From a misspent childhood, devoted almost entirely to the subject of soccer, I seemed to remember that when young Stanley Matthews made his debut at the age of seventeen, a local manager decided that the lad had no potential. 'Stanley Matthews lacks the big match temperament,' he said. 'He will never hold down a first team place in top class soccer.' Of course, quite apart from being the first English international ever to be knighted, Sir Stanley was still holding down a first team place in League Football at the age of fifty.

Michael then recalled the Hollywood anecdote of Fred Astaire and his first audition at MGM. The decision had been swift and definite: 'That guy has enormous ears, and a bad chin line. He'll never make it.'

That casting director's grandfather must have been the editor of the *San Francisco Examiner* in 1869, when Rudyard Kipling was sacked from his job as a cub reporter. The editor clearly had equal faith in his own judgement: 'I'm sorry, Mr Kipling,' he said, 'but you just don't know how to use the English language.'

The theme of bad decisions seemed to Michael and me to be an idea which might, in movie parlance, 'have legs'. Indeed, the movie world itself is full of examples. Charles Laughton turned down the role of the troubled colonel in *The Bridge on the River Kwai*, saying he didn't understand the role. Sir Alec Guinness didn't want the role much, either. He turned it down three times, and later tried to quit. Eventually, however, Charles Laughton said it all. He saw Guinness in the movie and remarked, '*Now* I

11

understand the role'. And then he kicked himself.

Louis B. Mayer was saved in the nick of time from what could have been a monumental bad decision. He rejected what he regarded as the ludicrous idea of Judy Garland playing Dorothy in *The Wizard of Oz*. 'Judy', said Mayer, 'is too old for Dorothy.' He wanted Shirley Temple for the part but fortunately for him and for us — and probably for Shirley — Judy prevailed.

Theatrical judgements and decisions can be equally eccentric. *Life with Father* reigned on Broadway for seven-and-a-half years from November 1939, becoming the longest-running play of its time with a total of 3,224 performances. However, no less an authority than Robert Benchley had not only read the script and dismissed it but told a prospective backer, 'I could smell it as the postman came whistling down the lane. Don't put a dime in it.'

And in 1956, twenty other potential investors were so unenthusiastic about a new musical based on a Shakespearian play, written by Leonard Bernstein, Stephen Sondheim, Arthur Laurents and Jerome Robbins, that impresario Cheryl Crawford decided the project was not for her. The play was *Romeo and Juliet* and the musical was, of course, *West Side Story*.

But these are just a few examples touching on some areas of human endeavour. What was the first bad decision, and where did it take place? I suppose that the location must have been the Garden of Eden and the perpetrators Adam and Eve.

'And when the woman saw that the tree was good for food, and that it was pleasant to the eyes, and a tree to be desired to make one wise, she took of the fruit thereof, and did eat, and gave also unto her husband with her; and he

12

did eat. And the eyes of them both were opened and they knew that they were naked.' *Genesis*, Chapter 3, vv. 6 & 7.

Unless you feel that the human race has made the optimum use of its expensively acquired wisdom, ability to go through life with its eyes open, and indeed of its nakedness, then that was clearly a bad decision.

At any rate, by the end of Chapter 3, Adam and Eve had been banished from the Garden of Eden and man's ability to make bad decisions had been recognised — and roundly cursed — by the Almighty. Indeed, the Old Testament is replete with further examples. Esau, an hairy man, and the son of Isaac and Rebecca, decided to sell his birthright to his brother Jacob for a mess of pottage, and very little good came of it. The inhabitants of the world decided to join together at Babel and build a tower as a stairway to Heaven. Owing to the absence of simultaneous translation, the project collapsed in confusion.

Biblical bad decisions were not confined to the Old Testament. Prior to starting his revolutionary Cable News Network in America, the colourful Atlanta entrepreneur, Ted Turner, told me: 'Of course in selecting staff I shall make a few bad decisions. After all, Jesus Christ only had to make twelve appointments and one of them was a bummer!' (The jury is still out on Mr Turner's own bold decision to launch CNN.)

The pattern has continued from Biblical times right up until the present day. In 1946, British Minister of Food John Strachey earmarked more than three million acres of Tanganyika, Northern Rhodesia and Kenya for an ambitious plan to grow protein-rich food to feed the war-devastated millions of Europe. In 1961 John F. Kennedy decided to allow 1500 exiles, equipped, trained and transported by the Americans, to return to their homeland and thus allow the freedom-loving people of Cuba to rise spontaneously and overthrow an unpopular tyrant palpably with no support. Each sounded like a good idea at the time, but the phrases 'Groundnut Scheme' and 'Bay of Pigs' have become synonymous with bad decisions of the first — or should it be the last? — magnitude.

Bad decisions, then, take many forms. (Indeed, we trust, gentle reader, that you will never come to regard buying this book as one of yours.) We tried to throw our net as wide as possible. Indeed, as an experiment — even, one might say, a bad decision — we advertised in the newspapers for prime examples of the genre. To our dismay, some seven hundred readers wrote to inform us that the worst decision ever made in this country was to allow immigration from the Commonwealth. A few even added helpfully that the *Empire Windrush* — the ship which brought the first immigrants from the West Indies — should have been torpedoed at sea. As the luckless vessel was sinking beneath the postal waves for about the seventeenth time, we decided to abandon this approach.

Barbara Twigg initiated more orthodox lines of research, and at the same time we talked to as many people as we could. While we were seeking bad decisions in general, not necessarily bad decisions from people's own experience, several nonetheless volunteered them. Jim Slater wryly recalled the moment when, dubbed by Fleet Street as the arch speculator, he turned down the opportunity to invest £1 million in North Sea Oil which would now be worth more than £100 million. His grounds? The investment was 'too speculative'. In terms of more general financial decision-making, he felt that the profoundly

14

inflationary way that decimalisation was implemented in this country has always been underestimated. There was, he said, a basic psychological error. Because the pound was chosen as the basic unit, the penny became too enhanced in value at precisely the moment its size was being reduced to relative insignificance.

As the editor and co-creator of the best-selling book in publishing history, *The Guinness Book of Records,* Norris McWhirter was able to regard with detached amusement a bad decision that almost was. When Arthur Guinness and Company's media experts — their advertising agents, S.H. Benson — heard about the book on superlatives that the company was contemplating, they demanded further information, and then delivered their professional judgement. The project was 'amateurish, inaccurate and would never catch on.' That was approximately forty-four million copies ago.

The first bad decision that came to John Aspinall's mind was one of his own. 'I sold the Clermont Club for £1 million back in 1972 before the Arab invasion began. It has made £5 million profit a year ever since.'

George Plimpton's favourite bad decision was not his own but General John Sedgwick's during the Battle of the Wilderness in the American Civil War. The good general was inspecting his troops and standing gazing out over a parapet. His officers urged him to duck down, but the general had scant respect for the enemy and decided to ignore the warnings.

'Nonsense,' he declared. 'They couldn't hit an elephant at this dist . . . .'

While checking with others, we also tried to dig into our own experience. For me, one of the clearest examples of a bad planning decision will always be the fourteen-storey Ronan Point in South London, and its chilling collapse in 1968. In one of its early attempts to reassure the public retroactively, the Ministry of Housing was talking cheerfully and encouragingly about the hundreds and thousands of buildings that had been put up in Scandinavia using the same Larsen-Neilson system. However, when we talked to Larsen-Nielson themselves in Copenhagen, we discovered that they had never built higher than eight storeys, something of which the Ministry seemed unaware. One reason why they hadn't built higher than eight storeys was that the Danish Ministry of Housing wouldn't let them. This was something else of which our Ministry of Housing was unaware. (In the case of Government Departments, there seems to be an almost direct mathematical ratio between the incidence of such public placebos and the magnitude of the bad decision to be obfuscated).

On January 13th, 1950 an Old Bailey jury made the tragically bad decision to convict Timothy Evans of the murder of his baby daughter, Geraldine, at 10 Rillington Place. Timothy Evans was hanged on March 9th, 1950. Over the years, a movement to pardon Timothy Evans grew up, and in the House of Commons the leading organiser of the petition to re-open the case was Opposition MP, Sir Frank Soskice. It is one of the bitter ironies of decision-making in Whitehall that when Sir Frank was appointed Home Secretary in the Labour Government one of his first duties was to reject his own petition when it was presented to him. It was 'contrary to Home Office Policy', he had been informed. (Sir Frank and the Home Office did, however, have second thoughts along the way and Timothy Evans was finally pardoned in November 1966.)

16

Michael Deakin was working in Leeds at the time that the West Yorkshire Police made their own tragically bad decision when they decided to focus the bulk of their campaign to find the Yorkshire Ripper on a man with a Wearside accent, following the receipt of that haunting, taunting tape. When asked if the police were certain that the mysterious voice was the Ripper's, Detective Chief Superintendent John Hobson had replied, 'One can never be one hundred per cent certain, but we are ninety-nine per cent.' While the police proceeded to spend upward of £1 million on advertising and publicity and countless police man-hours in the quest for the voice on the tape, Peter Sutcliffe remained at large.

When I interviewed the late Baldur von Schirach, former Head of the Hitler Youth, he was adamant. He knew what he regarded as the world's worst decision, 'We were very stupid, very stupid, Mr Frost, to stop attacking Britain and attack Russia.' He leant forward, his eyes narrowing, 'Because if we had continued attacking Britain, it would not have been very good for you, Mr Frost . . .'

That was a decisively bad decision, making its impact clearly felt on history. The chemistry between bad decisions and the events which follow them is not always so clear. Take for example the mistakes of the Shah of Iran. Clearly, there were a number of bad decisions. For example, in the autumn of 1978, as his reign was ebbing, the Shah found the peace of his realm much disturbed by an obscure mullah, the Ayatollah Khomeini. The Ayatollah had been exiled by the Shah and was based at a remote shrine at Najaq in Iraq, a country with which the Shah had been on bad terms. There are a limited number of five-star restaurants in Najaq, and few journalists felt impelled

17

to include them on their expense accounts, so the Ayatollah lived on unknown to the world at large. However, much against advice, the Shah pressured the Iraqis to expel the holy man, whom he wished to see harried at all costs.

The intention was that Khomeini should become a homeless exile, but he immediately went to Paris where, emerging from total obscurity, he embarked on a brilliant public relations campaign against the Shah, conducted in the full glare of the western press who hitherto hadn't even known what or who an Ayatollah was, and with the unspoken blessing of the French, who alone among the Western nations knew that, whatever his political condition, the Shah's medical condition was terminal. These mounting pressures played their part in the flow of events which culminated on January 17th, 1979 when the dynasty fell, and it was the Shah himself who became the 'Flying Dutchman.'

In truth, perhaps the Shah's deepest, most far-reaching bad decision was the most oft-repeated. It was his continual instruction to his security forces to concentrate on the only direction from which the threat could possibly come — the Left. The people of Iran, he told me in January 1978, had decided that they wished religion to have no place in political life. 'So if there was ever any clash between religion and the monarchy, the monarchy must win?' The Shah was indulgent about my Western lack of perception. 'Well, it would be very embarrassing if it were not so,' he smiled.

It was, of course, much worse than that — for him, and for his people. But if he had made all the right decisions, could he have withstood the dynamic of history? The 'if's are legion, the historical autopsy barely underway. The

Shah, alone with his speculations, in exile in Panama in January 1980, managed a rueful smile: 'When things go wrong, everything is a mistake.'

There is not necessarily any consistent correlation between the bad decisions in this book and their after-effects. In some cases, retribution was swift, even excessive. In other cases, the laughter of later generations is perhaps the first come-uppance for the perpetrators. The basic ingredients of the recipe for many of these bad decisions does not vary greatly, but the portions differ wildly. We find ourselves with an amalgam of mistakes, misjudgements, near-misses and 'should have known betters', a cocktail of pig-headedness, bone-headedness and wrong-headedness. Ideally, the connoisseur's bad decision should contain a liberal admixture of arrogance and a disregard for valid advice. As ever, the ancient Greeks had a word for it — even better, a god. They invented one — Nemesis — especially to punish bad decisions, although nobody seemed to know what he or she actually looked like. Perhaps the modern incarnation of the deity is a tax inspector, a parking meter attendant or Esther Rantzen. Being a tidy lot by and large, the Greeks also invented a way of keeping Nemesis away — or at least negating the terrible after-effects of a legendary bad decision. You spat on the ground — and the god pushed off. It may still be effective — but nobody these days seems to be trying it, except possibly Billy Connolly in his late-night dealings with press photographers.

There are certainly lessons to be learned from many of the bad decisions in this book. However, not even the most diligent care is necessarily a total protection. A little while ago, an aged and extremely distinguished don died in

19

Oxford. He received, as was appropriate, a lengthy and glowing obituary in *The Times*. After listing his many honours and accomplishments, the obituarist concluded: 'He agonised long and carefully over every decision in a long life — and then regretted just as bitterly the choices he had made.'

If such a painstaking scholar fared that way, what hope have we? Bad decisions are not the same as bad luck, but what we now regard as good decisions certainly needed their measure of good luck. That is why, however confident about the future of TV-AM I may be, I can but hope and pray that a future edition of this book will not contain an entry beginning: 'In 1980 David Frost stated that Britain was ready for Breakfast Television. "It is the last new frontier," he said. But just a few years later that new frontier . . . .' However much I have enjoyed preparing this book, and however much I hope you enjoy reading it, there have been many times when I have read a press clipping or piece of research and thought, 'There, but for the grace of God, goes . . . .'

David Frost

Prophet is a dirty word

In the year 480 BC Xerxes, King of Persia, decided to settle a long-running feud with the Greeks, and bury forever the Athenian Empire, which had given him trouble ever since they trounced him at Marathon. He planned to march his army from Asia into Europe across a bridge of pontoons which his engineers would build over the Hellespont. But, aware that this could be a risky venture, he first sought the advice of the Oracle at Delphi.

'If you cross the Hellespont,' he was told, 'a mighty Empire will fall.'

Being an optimist, Xerxes did not pause to consider that the Oracle already had a reputation for being 'delphic'. He interpreted her words as encouragement and pushed ahead with his plan. At first all went well and his armies overcame the Spartans at Thermopolyae; but then he was decisively defeated at the Battle of Salamis. At this point, presumably, it dawned on Xerxes that the Oracle hadn't specified *which* Empire would fall. It is not recorded whether the King kicked himself. He did, however, work off his hard feelings by ordering his executioner to give three hundred lashes to the water of the Hellespont.

Given this sort of track record, it is not surprising that Oracles and Prophets got themselves a bad reputation in the classical world and that five hundred years later the City Fathers of the Roman town of Pompeii decided to ignore the Sybils from the local temple when they warned of imminent disaster and urged that the town be evacuated.

The citizens of Pompeii were rationalists and reckoned that, with business only just recovering from a disastrous earthquake in 62 AD, the last thing they needed was this kind of scare story.

The Sybils, however, followed their own advice and left town. They were the only survivors when, next day, Mount Vesuvius erupted and buried Pompeii under a ten-foot layer of ash.

Being, in 1857, a fairly primitive people, the Gealeke Xhosa tribe of South Africa probably did not know of the sort of trouble that prophecies had caused to King Xerxes. So when a fourteen-year-old prophetess, one Nongqawuse, reported a vision she had seen in the waters of the River Gxara they were all too ready to heed her. She had seen, she told her fellow Xhosas, the faces of their dead elders staring up at her from the depths of the river. Moreover, she said, the meaning of the vision was perfectly clear: if the tribe wanted to regain its dead leaders, then they must slaughter all their livestock on or before February 18th 1857.

As a result of following this advice the entire tribe starved to death.

Anything to oblige

On February 18th, 1981, Mrs Dora Wilson looked out of her window in Harlow New Town and saw a group of men loading her neighbours' priceless collection of Persian carpets into a pantechnicon.

'What are you doing?' she called, knowing her neighbours were on holiday.

'We're taking them to be cleaned, Madam,' the men replied.

Quick as a flash Mrs Wilson decided to take advantage of the service they offered.

'Will you please take mine too?' she asked.

The men obliged. They were burglars.

This land is my land

The territorial expansion of the United States owed much to the courage and pioneering spirit of its citizens, but the contribution made by other people's mistakes was also considerable.

One of the first victims claimed by the talent for making a good deal which the New World inspired in its settlers was an anonymous Indian chief who, in 1626, sold the island of Manhattan to Governor Peter Minuit for $24 worth of axes, kettles and fabric.

A city block in mid-town Manhattan passes hands these days for around $80 million. Even allowing for inflation, Governor Minuit got himself a bargain.

In 1803 the Emperor Napoleon, who had his mind on European affairs at the time, decided to dispense with France's American possessions. He sold the entire Mississippi Valley, an area of 828,000 square miles, extending from Canada to the Gulf of Mexico and westward to the Rockies, to the infant American Republic. By this deal — the Louisiana Purchase as it was called — the American President, Thomas Jefferson doubled the size of his country, and the price was only $15 million.

On March 30th 1867 an agreement was made between Czar Alexander II of all the Russias and the American Secretary of State, Mr W.H. Seward, whereby the United States purchased the territory of Alaska. Surveying 'all the Russias', the Czar had decided that his empire could do without this remote, frozen and generally unpromising specimen, and he disposed of it for a mere $7.2 million.

His error became manifest nearly twenty years later when in 1896 gold was discovered in the territory. Alec McDonald, nicknamed King of the Klondike, hit pay dirt and parlayed his load into $20 million.

A century later 'black gold' — oil — was struck on Alaska's North Slope, and it became once more the scene of a stampede for mineral wealth.

One of the most short-sighted real estate deals of all time took place in November 1886, the day a gold prospector, Sors Hariezon, decided to sell a claim he had made on the farm of Gert Oosterhuizen at Witwatersrand in the Transvaal. The claim fetched £10, and Hariezon moved on.

Over the next ninety years the mines sunk on or near Hariezon's claim produced upwards of a million kilograms of gold per year — seventy per cent of the Western World's gold supply.

It should not, however, be thought that the mistake of selling the wrong bit of land at the wrong time and at the wrong price is all that exclusive to diplomats.

In January 1978, the Committee of the Royal Melbourne

Golf Club, faced with rising costs, decided to realise some of the Club's assets. Accordingly, they authorised the Secretary to sell some bushland which bordered on the course to a local speculative builder.

The Secretary muddled up the title deeds and sold off the 8th, 9th, 10th and 11th fairways of the Royal Melbourne. When the builder came to take possession of the site he had bought, he found the Australian Professional Golfers' Association championship in full swing.

London Calling

When one of the stalwart BBC doormen retired recently the occasion was marked by a party. The doorman had given nearly half a century of service to the Corporation — he was even reputed to have been on cordial terms with Lord Reith — and many colleagues gave generously to a collection for his parting presentation.

At the party he was duly presented with a digital watch — a present totally appropriate in all but one respect. Like many BBC employees in his section, the doorman had been disabled in the war and, while he had a left wrist on which to bear the watch, he had no right hand with which to press the 'on' button.

The lack of foresight on the BBC's part can have come as no surprise to anyone who had worked for the Corporation during the 1950s when the New Broadcasting House was built. The corridors connecting the old building to the new one are labyrinthine and extremely narrow. The Music Department became concerned about the difficulties they would face in transporting their Bechstein Grand Pianos from one concert room to another, and decided upon a series of trials to find the easiest route.

They asked the BBC carpenters to mock up a full-size piano in plywood for the purpose, rather than risk permanently blocking the corridors with a finely tuned

and expensive instrument. The model was duly constructed — and was found to be too large to pass through
the doors of the woodwork shop.

Prohibition

Oh, what a lovely war

In the spring of 1914 Colonel Apis Dimitrievic, leader of the Serbian terrorist gang, the Black Hand, decided to arm a group of young patriots, led by Gavrilo Princip, who planned to assassinate the Archduke Franz Ferdinand of Austria during a visit to Sarajevo in Bosnia. The indirect consequences of this decision were impressive:

The Archduke and his wife were assassinated on June 28th, 1914.

On July 23rd the Austro-Hungarian Empire issued an ultimatum to Serbia.

July 26th:	Austria mobilised on the Russian Front.
July 28th:	The Austro-Hungarian Empire declared war on Serbia.
August 1st:	Germany declared war on Russia. France mobilised. Italy declared her neutrality.
August 2nd:	Germany occupied Luxembourg. Germany issued an ultimatum to Belgium.
August 4th:	Britain declared war on Germany. US declared her neutrality.
August 5th:	Austria-Hungary declared war on Russia.

August 6th:	Serbia and Montenegro declared war on Germany.
August 10th:	France declared war on Austria.
August 12th:	Britain declared war on Austria-Hungary.
August 15th:	Japan issued an utlimatum to Germany.
August 28th:	Austria-Hungary declared war on Belgium.

The world was at war. The only great power not embroiled in the indirect consequences of the Black Hand's action was the United States. But a year later Kapitan-Lieutenant Walter Schweiger put that right. He was at the time commanding the submarine U—20. Spotting the British liner SS *Lusitania* off the Irish coast on May 7th, 1915, he decided to follow the recent decision of the German High Command and torpedo her without warning.

Among the 1200 passengers on board the *Lusitania* who perished with the ship were 128 Americans. Their deaths were instrumental in bringing the US into the war against Germany.

If wars break out that easily in the West, then in excitable Latin America it's even worse.

In the nineteenth century, the military triumphs of Napoleon Bonaparte made such an impact all over the world that quite large numbers of deranged people came to believe that they were the great Emperor. In most cases this delusion was relatively harmless; but, unfortunately, one victim was the President of Paraguay, Francisco Solano Lopez. He resolved to demonstrate the truth of his conviction in the most practical possible way and, on

18th March 1865, he declared war on the neighbouring states of Uruguay, Brazil and Argentina — thus setting himself a challenge worthy of a military genius.

Señor Lopez' misapprehension about his own identity cost the lives of half his fellow citizens over the subsequent five years, as well as a complete breakdown of all social and political institutions.

A hundred years later, a similar excitability still prevailed. On June 27th 1969 the referee awarded a late penalty to El Salvador in their World Cup football match against their neighbour Honduras. El Salvador scored from the penalty spot, and won the match 3-2 — the decider in three fiercely contested draws between the teams.

When news of the result spread, wild, jingoistic riots swept through both capital cities as fans re-fought the match on the streets, looting and beating up the opposition supporters. On July 3rd, as a direct result, war broke out between the two countries.

Two thousand soldiers of both nations were slain before peace was restored, and the Central American Common Market, crucial to both economies, came to an end. As a result both Honduras and El Salvador suffered serious food shortage.

El Salvador was eliminated in the next round of the World Cup.

Sorry, right number

In January 1971 while Dr Milton Obote, leader of Uganda, was attending the Commonwealth Prime Ministers Conference in Singapore, he decided to dismiss one of Uganda's senior Army Officers, Brigadier-General Amin.

Dr Obote determined to act on his decision at once and asked his hotel to connect him with the Army Chief of Staff in Lusaka. The telephone operator in Uganda, a member of the Lua tribe, decided that his fellow tribesman, General Amin, would be interested in the Prime Minister's news and put the call through to Amin. Rather than accept redundancy, Amin took immediate action.

Which is not to say that telegrams cannot have equally dire results. For instance, at the very end of the last war the Allies issued the Potsdam telegram, demanding that the Imperial Japanese armies surrender forthwith. The Japanese Government at once responded with an announcement that it was withholding immediate comment on the ultimatum pending 'deliberations' by the Imperial Government.

Unfortunately the official Japanese Government News Agency, in the heat of issuing this critical statement in English, decided to translate the Japanese word which means 'withholding comment for the time being' as 'deliberately ignore'.

Believing the ultimatum had been rejected, President Truman most reluctantly authorised the A-bomb attacks on Hiroshima and Nagasaki.

Change of flight plan

In June 1977, James Barthes, a South African hang-gliding instructor, spotted an interesting sight and decided to make an obscene gesture at Mrs Francis Chapman who was sunbathing naked on a rooftop below his flight path.

Her husband came out of the bedroom armed with a sub-machine gun and blasted the bird man out of the sky.

FOR GOD'S SAKE — NOT BEFORE AUGUST THE TWELTH !

Model miscalculations

In 1948 the Volkswagen factory was inspected by British and American experts who were asked to evaluate the possibilities of taking it over as a contribution to war reparations. The factory's sole product was the 'Beetle', designed before the war as a 'peoples' car' for German workers. The experts' task, therefore, amounted to assessing the Beetle's chances in the postwar market place.

The American delegation was led by Ernest Breech, President of the Ford Motor Company. His verdict was 'the car is not worth a damn.' Sir William Rootes, for the British, took a similar view: 'The Volkswagen,' he said, 'does not meet the fundamental technical requirements of a motor car.'

Having dismissed the Volkswagen, the Ford Motor Company turned its mind in due course to devising the kind of car which it thought it could sell, one that was 'perfectly geared to American taste.' The new science of market research was employed to make sure that absolutely everything was right with the vehicle and its marketing, even down to the name — the Edsel, a traditional Ford-family Christian name.

Ford dealers were less than enthusiastic about the Edsel when it was presented to them, but Ford's were still confident they had a winner — how could a vehicle upon which so much skill and talent, and so many dollars, had been lavished, fail?

As it turned out, very easily. The public shared the dealers' opinion, the car went out of production after two years, two months and fifteen days and $350 million short of the point at which its makers could expect to see a profit.

If Ford's mistake with the Edsel was complex and mysterious, one of the disasters which befell their arch-rivals, General Motors, was magnificently straightforward. In the early 1960s they launched their new 'compact' Chevrolet Nova model in the Mexican market. It was only when the appallingly bad sales figures came in that someone in Detroit remembered that *no va* means 'no go' in Spanish.

In 1966 General Motors dropped another memorable clanger. The corporation had been increasingly irritated by the activities of an obscure young consumer-rights activist called Ralph Nader who had pursued an effective campaign against GM's Corvair model which he described as 'unsafe at any speed'. Rather than investigate the deficiencies of their car, GM thought it would be easier and cheaper to investigate Mr Nader, in the hope that his private life or financial dealings would prove to include something to his discredit.

When Nader discovered that he was being followed by detectives employed by General Motors, he sued the firm. His victory in the courtroom and the landmark award of $450,000 in damages gave the consumer movement the boost it needed to transform it into a force which would, over the coming years, cost the American automobile industry many millions of dollars.

However, for most dedicated motorists there is one bad decision which dwarfs all others. It was committed almost lightly in July 1935 by the City Fathers of Oklahoma City when, after lunch one day, they resolved to introduce a device which the town clerk christened 'a parking meter'.

The Crusades

THINK OF THIS AS A
DEEPLY MOVING
RELIGIOUS EXPERIENC.

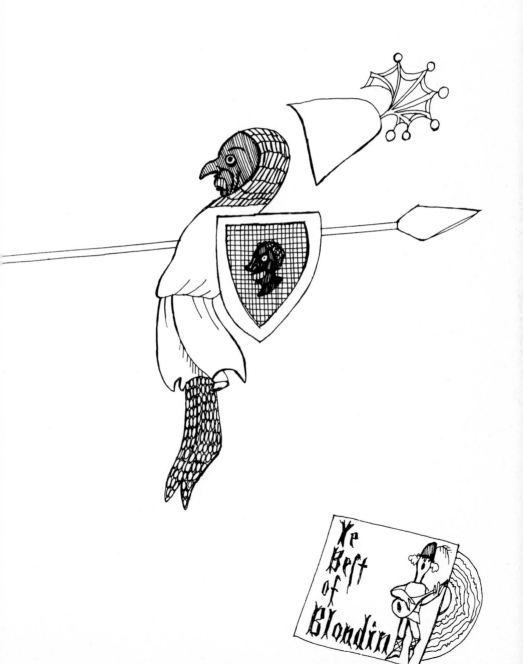

The body
in question

In 1910 Olav Olavson, a Swedish citizen, fell upon hard times and decided to sell his body for medical research after his death to the Karolinska Institute in Stockholm.

The following year he inherited a fortune and resolved to buy himself back. The Institute refused to sell its rights to his body, went to court and won possession of it. Moreover, the Institute obtained damages, since Olav had had two teeth pulled out without asking their permission as ultimate owners of his body.

RE YOUR TRANSFER, LAD, WE
HAVE SOLD YOUR BODY TO SCIENCE

A little learning

In 1930 the LCC employed Cyril Burt as their Chief Educational Psychologist. Sir Cyril's major contribution to science had been his research on identical twins which seemed to confirm the belief that intelligence is inherited and not acquired.

It therefore followed that there was no point in keeping children together in school, since the less bright would hold back the intelligent. Accordingly it was decided to institute the 'Eleven Plus Exam', by which children were irrevocably streamed at an early age according to ability.

After his death it was found that Sir Cyril had forged his research, and lied and cheated to prevent his being discovered. (News seems to travel slowly in conservative academic circles — one primary school in Surrey is still called the 'Sir Cyril Burt School'.)

Very often, alas, those set to teach the young are not as perceptive or far-sighted as they believe themselves to be.

For instance, when on June 22, 1832, the young Guiseppi Verdi applied to study music at the Royal and Imperial Conservatoire of Milan, the principal, Maestro Professor Francesco Basily, rejected the boy on the grounds he was 'over-age — and certain to prove mediocre.'

In 1854 the Professor of Literature at the Lycée d'Aix decided to take the unprecedented step of awarding one of his pupils nought for composition and French literature. The pupil's name was Emile Zola.

On July 12 1880 H.O.D. Davidson, a housemaster at Harrow, wrote a considered opinion of one of his pupils. 'He is forgetful, careless, unpunctual, irregular in every way . . . . If he is unable to conquer this slovenliness he will never make a success of public school.' The boy, he added, was bottom of his class. Fortunately Winston Churchill turned out to be a late developer.

Even pure genius of the most elevated sort is no protection against the teaching profession at its worst. Consider what happened in 1898 when the young Albert Einstein applied for admission to the Munich Technical Institute. The young genius was turned down on the grounds that he 'showed no promise'. Denied the scientific education he sought, Einstein was forced to work first as a postman and then as an inspector in the Swiss Patent Office in Berne. He did, while in the latter job, however, manage to teach himself enough about physics to formulate the theory of relativity.

Finally, how about this as an example of learned blindness? To resounding academic plaudits, in 1908 the astronomer Percival Lowell announced at his observatory in Flagstaff, Arizona, that he had discovered canals on Mars. These, he further related in his book *Mars as the Abode of Life*, were red and seemed mysteriously to move. He succeeded, however, in charting them and detailed maps were issued and included in school atlases throughout the world.

There are no canals on Mars. The great astronomer was, in fact, suffering from a rare eye disease — now known as Lowell's Syndrome — the symptom of which is to see the veins of one's own eyes.

So eminent was Lowell that none dared contradict him.

Literary criticism

There are a few things that more people have been wrong about more often than books.

Take the Nobel Prize for Literature for example. When the first prize was awarded in 1901, among other great writers, Henrik Ibsen, Henry James, Emile Zola and Joseph Conrad were all still alive. With a perversity which has been followed by most of their successors, the committee awarded the first Nobel Prize for Literature to the French novelist René Sully-Prudhomme. Next year, in 1902, they decided to give the cash-rich reward to Theodor Mommsen; in 1903 to Björnstjerne Björnson; in 1904 to Frederic Mistral, a poet who wrote in Provençal dialect; in 1905 they decided on Henryk Sienkiewicz; and the next year to Giosue Carducci. In 1907 they had especially long deliberations and decided to give that year's Prize to Rudyard Kipling. The next year it went to Rudolf Eucken. In 1909 the Swedish Academy decided on its first female Laureate — Selma Ottiliana Lovisa Lagerlof; and the 1910 award went to the German lyric poet Paul von Heyse.

In that year, on November 10th, Leo Tolstoy, author among much else of *War and Peace* and *Anna Karenina*, died. He had been nominated repeatedly for the Nobel Prize, which he had much desired — and had been passed over ten times.

In 1900, Miss Beatrix Potter, a London spinster with a penchant for painting watercolours of toadstools, wrote and illustrated a children's book which she called *Peter Rabbit*. She sent text and illustrations to six publishers, all of whom rejected it.

Being a lady of independent means and spirit, Miss Potter persevered. She had the book privately printed at the end of 1901, and sold copies to friends and relatives. One of the publishers who had earlier turned the book down, Frederick Warne, saw one of these copies and decided that it did after all have some possibilities. He did not, however, allow his enthusiasm to run away with him. Warne's would handle the book, they told the author, but only on condition that she would bear the financial risks. Three years later sales had topped 75,000 copies and already, Messrs Warne were beginning to realise the scale of their error.

Miss Potter was a good deal more fortunate than some literary ladies. In 1836 one of their number wrote to the eminent critic and man of letters Robert Southey, submitting a short sample of her work and asking his advice on the advisability of trying to earn her living by writing.

Three months later he replied: 'Literature cannot be the business of a woman's life, and it ought not to be. The more she is engaged in her proper duties, the less leisure will she have for it, even as an accomplishment and recreation. To those duties you have not yet been called, and when you are you will be less eager for celebrity.'

So discouraged was Ms Charlotte Bronte by this negative advice that for ten years she scarcely put pen to paper.

After surveying the catalogue of publishing errors which follow, the compilers of this book began to feel that it is a distinctly bad sign that it was accepted by the first publisher who saw it. Various book publishers have decided over the years that the following books were uncommercial or lacking in literary merit:

M.A.S.H. — turned down by twenty-one publishers.
Lorna Doone — turned down by eighteen publishers.
The Silent Spring — turned down by five publishers.
Jonathan Livingston Seagull — turned down by eighteen publishers.
Kon Tiki — turned down by twenty publishers.
The Peter Principle — turned down by sixteen publishers.

In February 1970 Frederick Forsyth, who had recently left the BBC News Department, submitted the manuscript of a thriller he had written to the publishers W.H. Allen. Eight weeks later they returned it, declining to publish it since it 'had no reader interest'.

Cassells, Collins, Michael Joseph and Hutchinsons also passed it up. Then Hutchinsons thought again, and eventually agreed to publish it. To date, *The Day of the Jackal* has sold 8 million copies.

Adventure is clearly a dangerous commodity. In the annals of the Oxford University Press there is a note reading: 'Capt. W.E. Johns is asking for ten guineas for his next Biggles story. This is outrageous. Let him place it elsewhere.'

Just occasionally, however, publishers get their own back. For instance, on 1st June 1938 there appeared the first issue of 'Action Comics' which introduced to the world the character of Superman. It was the creation of Joe Shuster and Jerry Siegel who, believing that a birdman in the hand was worth two in the bush, decided to sell all rights in the character they had devised to their publishers for the sum of $130 — $65 each.

Artistic criticism

Around 1550, the Duke Lorenzo de Medici decided that he did not like the great murals by Leonardo da Vinci depicting the Battle of Anghiari which decorated the walls of the Palazzo Vecchio in Florence. These paintings, the Duke reasoned, were unfashionable in style and politically undesirable, having been painted under the earlier Republican regime.

He therefore decided to commission the diarist, gossip-writer and fifth-rate painter, Giorgio Vasari, to obliterate Leonardo's works and replace them with compositions of his own.

Today, more than a million dollars is being spent trying to undo Duke Lorenzo's handiwork, and uncover Leonardo's masterpiece once more.

The smoke
gets in your eyes

At the turn of the century the firm of E.G. Alton & Co of Derby Road, Nottingham, was in the cigar-making business. One day its proprietor was approached by a neighbour and competitor with the suggestion that the two firms should go into partnership and manufacture a new kind of smoking material consisting of finely chopped tobacco wrapped in paper — a 'cigar-ette'.

Mr Alton was unimpressed and declined the proposal. 'Your cigar-ettes will never become popular,' he told his rival, a certain John Player.

Mr Player, and his imitators, were in fact so successful that their product became a serious threat to the nation's health. By 1977 even the cigarette industry itself recognised the problem and spent millions developing new brands of cigarettes containing tobacco substitutes which would be both cheaper and safer than the real thing.

However, the Government decided that if the manufacturers were permitted to advertise the real benefits of their new cigarettes, more people would take up smoking. They therefore recommended that the new brands should carry the same health warning as existing ones and that they should be taxed just as heavily.

Eleven brands of tobacco-substitute cigarettes were put on the market; having no apparent advantage, as far as the smoker could discover from the packet, they all flopped disastrously. Vast bonfires had to be made to dispose of the non-carcinogenic tobacco substitutes.

There are other, less common, ways in which smoking can damage your health.

In August 1981 Mr Frederick Burness was admitted to Colindale Hospital in North London suffering from acute bronchitis. He was placed in an oxygen tent.

Once settled in, despite repeated warnings, he decided he was desperate for a smoke, and reached for a packet of cigarettes and a lighter.

The oxygen tent, and Mr Burness, exploded together.

Danger-
men at work

In 1978 a gang of workmen engaged in maintenance work on the Chesterfield canal near Retford dredged up the end of a massive iron chain. Deciding that it represented a hazard to navigation, the foreman attached the chain to a winch on their boat and reeled it in. Conscious of a morning's work well done, the gang then took their lunchbreak. On returning to their vessel at 2.35 pm the workers found it sitting high and dry on the canal bed. They had, literally, pulled the plug out.

But such impetuousness is overshadowed by that of an American oil man, Mr Robert McCulloch. In April 1968, learning that London Bridge was to be demolished and replaced by a more modern design, McCulloch purchased it, sight unseen, for $1 million and had the dismantled structure shipped to Lake Havasu City, Arizona. Mr McCulloch expected the sight of this old-world landmark in its new setting to become a major tourist attraction.

Only when several thousand tons of stonework had arrived in Arizona and had been erected in the desert, did Mr McCulloch realise that London Bridge was not Tower Bridge. Instead of the picturesque gothic towers and opening centre span which he'd thought he was buying,

58

he'd got a perfectly ordinary-looking bridge which no tourist in his right mind would drive five miles to see.

At least Mr McCulloch still has a perfectly good bridge. It is a great deal harder to rebuild a Grade Two listed Georgian mansion like Manspath Hall near Solihull. Yet, thanks to Mr Paddy Keenan, that is what will have to be done if we are ever to see the house's famous portico again.

Mr Keenan was a director of a firm of demolition contractors, Danny Doyle of Birmingham, who had been hired to demolish a few derelict outbuildings. In order to give Mr Keenan a head start on his day's work, the company had delivered his bulldozer to the site the previous night and, finding a convenient driveway next to the mansion, parked it there. Being more of a man of action than an enthusiast for Georgian architecture, Mr Keenan, arriving on the site the next morning and feeling the urge to get his bulldozer blade into something meaty, did not trouble to consult the plans in his pocket which showed the work to be done. To him it was self-evident that if the bulldozer had been parked next to a Georgian mansion, then it was the mansion that required demolition.

He set to work with a will. When local residents protested he dismissed them robustly: 'Clear off,' he cried, 'I've got a job to do.' By the time the police had been summoned and arrived on the scene all that remained of Manspath Hall was a heap of rubble.

Not so
common markets

One slogan which the advertising and marketing world has spectacularly failed to absorb is 'When in Rome, do as the Romans do.' On the contrary, advertising executives are quite prepared to spend large amounts of money to persuade the Romans and everyone else to do as Madison Avenue does. As the following examples show, there are some things even advertising cannot achieve.

In the 1950s the Pepsodent Corporation undertook an aggressive export drive for their toothpaste in South East Asia. Reasoning that what worked in the United States would surely work in this new market, they based their advertising campaign on their tried and tested slogan: 'You'll wonder where the yellow went, when you brush your teeth with Pepsodent.'

Today it might be questioned whether this was the most tactful way of promoting a product in a market where most consumers were not noted for their Nordic complexions; but a Vice President of the Corporation who went out to investigate why the campaign had resulted in negligible sales found a more esoteric cause. Many natives of South East Asia chew betelnut, just as natives of the US chew gum. Betelnut, however, is more expensive than gum and also stains the teeth of the chewer. Accordingly, blackened teeth are a prized symbol of affluence and there was little demand for a product which promised to make the betel-chewer's consumption inconspicuous.

In 1960 the Imperial Tobacco Company launched a new brand of cigarette. Their marketing experts did much research and investigation and decided that the brand would be christened 'Strand' and would be launched on the market with the slogan 'You're never alone with a Strand'. The commercials which incorporated this slogan featured a solitary and enigmatic gentleman, usually in the pouring rain, finding solace for his isolation in a cigarette.

Unsurprisingly, the public decided that if people who smoked Strand spent their time standing about in the wet cut dead by their fellow men, then they wanted none of it. Sales of Strand were notably disastrous.

GOD IT'S LONELY WITH A STRAND!

In 1958 the giant American Campbell Soup Corporation felt that the time had come to market its product in Europe. In spite of advice to the contrary, it decided that the US and European markets must be identical and resolved simply to ship several million cans of its condensed soups for sale in the UK.

Almost none were sold — a considerable financial catastrophe. British housewives, it transpired, had no experience of condensed soups, and simply thought that Campbells soups were an over-priced US import in tiny cans.

In 1963 the American manufacturers of quality beds, Simmons & Co, decided to launch a major export drive in Japan.

After four years they reported a whopping loss.

Before opening in Japan, Simmons had simply not realised that the Japanese do not sleep on beds at all, let alone imported American beds, but on *futons*, a sort of mat.

Keep right on to the end of the road

In May 1981 Mr and Mrs Thomas Eltham decided to take a day trip from Dover to Boulogne. They hugely enjoyed their sightseeing and shopping but, not being able to speak the French tongue or read the street signs, when they wandered away from the town centre they soon became lost.

'We walked and walked,' said Mrs Eltham, 'and eventually night fell. Several people gave us lifts. Finally we reached the railway station.'

In despair the Elthams here decided to take a train from Boulogne SNCF to Paris.

'The ticket to Paris took most of our money,' said Mrs Eltham later. 'But when we got off at the station we found we were in Luxembourg, and not, as we had thought, in Paris. Furthermore, it was by now Tuesday morning and not, as we had hoped, only Monday night.'

The Luxembourg police, however, proved most obliging — they put the Elthams back on the train to Paris. The intrepid, but by now exhausted, couple fell asleep — only too soundly.

'When we woke up,' said Mrs Eltham, 'the signs outside the window said Basel. The Swiss police sent us back to

France and the French police at Belfort on the frontier said we should go to Montbeliard and there catch the Boulogne connection.'

The Elthams decided to walk the fifteen miles to Montbeliard where a charitable town council lodged them free in a hostel while they attempted to contact their family and friends in Blighty. But alas, owing to the complexities of the French telephone service, they merely got wrong numbers, or the engaged tone, or their friends appeared to be out. The Elthams therefore decided to get a job in order to earn enough money to buy two tickets to Boulogne. But Montbeliard is in an area of high unemployment and the non-French speaking Elthams were unable to find employment suited to their many talents.

Finally the local police gave them a travel warrant to Belfort — the frontier town they had started out from a week earlier. 'It was dark when we reached Belfort,' said Mrs Eltham, 'and somehow or other we lost our way. In the end we decided to walk the sixty-two kilometers to Vesoul. Then our luck changed. A lorry driver gave us a lift. We stayed in Vesoul a few days and then took the metro into Paris.'

By now the Elthams were really anxious to get home, so they made their way to the Gare du Nord, intent on taking a train. Unfortunately they misread the platform notices and the one they boarded went to Bonn.

With characteristic efficiency the German police simply ran the wanderers back over the French frontier.

'This time,' said the Elthams, 'things turned out for the best. A French policeman actually drove us to Boulogne where we spent twenty-four hours with the customs authorities.'

Finally the Elthams arrived at Dover. The immigration authorities decided to overlook their rather extended 'passportless day trip' and not to exercise their undoubted powers of arrest.

Penniless and exhausted, the Elthams walked the last twenty-three miles home.

'The previous year we had gone to the Isle of Wight,' said Mr Eltham when relating his shattering experience. 'We shall not be going abroad in future.'

Hot airplanes

There seems to be something about aircraft projects which makes politicians bite like fish presented with nice fat worms. Except, of course, that it's usually the taxpayers who find themselves floundering on the sharp financial hook, as in the case of the Concorde project at £1000 million, which even one of the present compilers would regretfully have to admit amounts to an unwarrantedly generous government subsidy towards his personal travel.

In 1930, Lord Thomson of Darlington was the Secretary of State for Air, and his great enthusiasm was the British airship, the R101. So much so that he decided to grace her maiden voyage to India, despite the fact that the great craft had not completed her trials and had no certificate of airworthiness.

'The R101 is as safe as a house,' he proclaimed as he climbed aboard. He was among the twenty-eight killed when, in the early hours of the following morning, the giant airship crashed into a hill near Beauvois.

In an effort to avoid mistakes like this after the Second World War, the Attlee Government decided to appoint a Committee under Lord Brabazon of Tara to decide what aircraft the British industry should build to meet the needs of the future. Even for an official body, the Brabazon Committee notched up a remarkable record.

After long and careful deliberation, they decided to build an aircraft large enough to link the far-flung British Empire (on which they knew the sun would never set) and slow enough to take off and land on primitive air strips in remote corners of the world. The result was the largest flying white elephant in history. The piston-powered Brabazon, as the plane was called, was so slow that its cruising speed was no faster than a 1930's bi-plane, and so large that its frame cracked under its own weight. Furthermore, the advent of the jet engine — a British invention — made the whole project obsolete before it was complete. When the Brabazon was scrapped at a cost of £12.5 million, it had never carried a fare-paying passenger.

Mindful of the glorious tradition of the Brabazon Committee, in 1957 the British Minister of Defence, Duncan Sandys, published his Department's revolutionary White Paper on the future of Britain's forces. In the years to come, the document confidently explained, manned aircraft would become obsolete, and all the tasks they performed would be left to the guided missiles which were the weapons of the future.

As a result, large numbers of projected aircraft were cancelled, and money and effort was concentrated on missiles such as 'Blue Streak'.

Mr Sandys' forecast turned out to be premature. In the next two decades the Royal Air Force had to spend thousands of millions of pounds on manned aircraft, many of them, perforce, American since their British counterparts had been cancelled. It was left to succeeding administrations to cancel most of the missile projects in which the White Paper had put its trust.

It is not just British and American politicians who suffer from this fatal infatuation with expensive flying machines. In 1956 it was decided to re-equip the West German Luftwaffe which was 'totally out of date'. As Federal Minister of Defence it fell to Franz Josef Strauss to make the choice of plane.

Given that the main requirement was for a low-level ground attack aircraft, it is, perhaps, curious that Herr Strauss's choice fell upon the Lockheed Corporation's F104 Starfighter, which had been designed specifically as a high altitude interceptor fighter. But Lockheed promised the Germans that the plane could be redesigned as a fighter-bomber which would then do everything they required. The price of the planes, it was agreed, would be cost plus eight per cent — expected to amount to £170,000 per plane.

In the event, the Germans had to pay about £700,000 for each of the F104 G's they received. But the price was the least of the problems. The redesigning produced a plane which was overweight and unstable and particularly prone to attempt, at low level and without warning, to loop the loop. Luftwaffe pilots quickly came to dread the aircraft which, as losses of planes and pilots escalated, was christened, 'the widow-maker' and 'the flying coffin'.

On October 15th 1980 the 195th German Starfighter crashed in a wood near Cologne. 'How do you get a Starfighter?', ran a current Luftwaffe joke. The answer: 'Buy a field and wait.'

Trial and error

On April 9th 1626 Francis Bacon climbed Highgate Hill, having decided upon a scientific experiment.

Here he ate a goose stuffed with snow, to see whether the ice had halted the natural decay of the flesh.

He died of typhoid.

Ah, well, back to ye death-bed

Conflict of interests

Back in the days when cricketers were divided into 'gentlemen' — who played for their own enjoyment — and 'players' — who played for their wages — the latter already relied, in the absence of a pension, upon the proceeds of their 'benefit' match to sustain them in their declining years.

In 1907 the Middlesex bowler Albert Trott was on the verge of retirement, and it was decided that his team's fixture against Somerset would be Trott's benefit match. In his zeal to end his career with a bang, Trott took four Somerset wickets with five balls, and went on to achieve another hat-trick — all in the same innings. Not surprisingly, the three-day match was over in a matter of hours and the takings at the gate, and thus Trott's benefit, proved negligible. Indeed, as he bowled his last over the other players heard him mutter prophetically, 'I am bowling myself into the workhouse.'

Another popular athlete of an earlier age at least *tried* to take better care of Number One. In 1898 a famous Turkish wrestler, Yousouf Ishmaelo, toured America with great commercial success.

In spite of the pleas of his managers and backers, he decided not to entrust his winnings to any other hand but his own, and converted the money into gold ingots which he carried in a belt wherever he went.

Eventually he decided to return to his native Turkey to enjoy his hard-earned savings. En route the vessel he was travelling on, the *Burgoyne*, struck a reef and was holed below the waterline.

Though the other passengers survived the wreck, even Ishmaelo's wrestler physique was unequal to the task of keeping a large quantity of gold bullion afloat. He went down with the ship.

Own goal

All credit to François Mitterand for his election to the French Presidency in 1981 — but did he get a little help from his opponent?

In 1973, 1974 and again in 1975, the incumbent President Valéry Giscard d'Estaing accepted gifts of a 'pipe' of diamonds from the Emperor Bokassa of the Central African Empire, whose few engaging habits included addressing Giscard as 'Papa'.

The satirical weekly *Canard Enchainé* found out and published the story. After much prevarication, Giscard said the gifts had *'Ni la forme, ni la valeur'* of the *Canard*'s allegations and claimed that they had been deposited in state museums.

The *Canard* checked. No deposits had been made.

Giscard then went on television and claimed, in the middle of the 1980 Presidential Election Campaign, that the diamonds had been sold and the money given to the Central African Red Cross.

The *Canard* checked. No gifts.

Giscard then claimed that they had been sent to President Drako, Bokassa's successor, only a few weeks earlier, destined for the Red Cross.

The *Canard* checked. Giscard had sent 114,997 francs, the equivalent of £10,000 — or, they estimated, one small diamond.

As Giscard left the Elysée Palace on foot, after his

♫ DIAMONDS
ARE A MAN'S
WORST ENEMY

defeat in 1981, a crowd surrounded him crying: 'Give back the diamonds! Give back the diamonds!'

Another tale of the way politicians boot the ball into their own net comes from Britain. At the end of the First World War, the British upper-classes reacted against four years of horror and austerity with a flamboyant fling of high-living and free-spending. This wave of extravagance and materialism much offended Stanley Baldwin, the future Prime Minister, who felt strongly that the rich should set an example of thrift and public spiritedness.

Accordingly, Mr Baldwin, who was Chancellor, advocated a voluntary levy on the wealthy to raise something like £50 million a year. On the principle of putting his money where his mouth was, he undertook to set an example by giving a quarter of his own assets back to the nation. He invested the sum in government stock and then burnt the certificates thus, in effect, making a gift to the Exchequer. His *beau geste* cost him £120,000. Nobody followed his example.

But perhaps the most decisive own goal of British history took place in 1745. Charles Edward Stuart, Bonnie Prince Charlie, had landed in the Hebrides and raised his banner. All Scotland rallied to him, Edinburgh fell and his armies marched south.

On December 6th, at Derby, a council of war was held at which the Prince, under heavy pressure from his advisors, decided to turn back rather than march on London where, unbeknownst to the Prince, his Hanoverian rival had already packed his belongings, reckoning his throne lost.

When the astonishing news that the Stuart armies had turned back reached London, the Hanoverians unpacked and sent an army under 'Butcher' Cumberland in hot pursuit of the Bonnie Prince and his highlanders. On April 16th, 1746 he caught them at Culloden.

But the 'Order of the Golden Boot' must go to a rather less romantic figure — Richard Milhous Nixon — for his decision to order voice-activated Sony Type TK50 tape recorders for the Oval Office in the White House.

The resulting tapes, he believed, would ensure his role in history.

They did.

A nose for news

Not all the press came well out of Watergate.

In 1974 the owner of the *San Francisco Chronicle*, Charles Thierot, turned down the syndication rights of a series of articles the Washington *Post* was running on the subject of an unexplained break-in at the Democratic headquarters in the Watergate Hotel.

'There will be no West Coast interest in the story', he said, letting his rival, the *Examiner*, pick up the rights for 500 dollars.

The smack of firm management

In 1965 the American Celanese Corporation decided to go into the paper business in Europe. It accordingly acquired an enormous plantation of eucalyptus trees in Sicily, intending to use them for pulp.

The trees safely acquired, the Celanese Corporation proceeded to the construction of a mill. This went up at record speed, and a keen and hitherto unemployed workforce was taken on.

Only when the expert management team arrived from the US to put the mill into production did somebody go to visit the plantations to see the raw material. They found it was composed entirely of freshly planted trees, only a few inches high, and totally useless for paper production for at least a generation.

Pulp had to be imported from Canada to keep the mill running in the interim twenty years or so.

The year after this debacle, Celanese losses exceeded 77 million dollars.

So much for firm management, transatlantic style. But things are much the same in backward Europe. Some years ago an ultra-modern thrusting conglomerate added a safari and wild-life park to its portfolio of interests.

From the outset the new regime decided to improve on the facilities and profitability. Scarcely was the ink dry on the contract than, running its businesslike eye down the accounts, Management lit upon a large item for oranges and bananas. 'It is out of season — these fruits are far too expensive for mere animals. In future let them eat swedes,' it was decreed. The poor beasts in question, however, came from verdant jungles in which fruit was never out of season and could no more digest swedes than they could stones. They wilted rapidly, and the policy had to be discarded.

Evolution 1: Firm Management 0

On the facilities front, it was decided to build an otter pool to cash in on the public love of the little furry mammals created by a then-current film *Ring of Bright Water*. A princely pool was constructed for the otters to plash in, and a well-known firm of animal suppliers was contracted to provide the new inmates.

Unfortunately, when they arrived the otters simply went to sleep in their deep and private burrows, refusing to gambol or entertain anybody.

Expert advice was summoned — and spoke. Management had been unlucky, and bought the worst sort of otter. All otters prefer the night; this kind refuses to move even a paw by day. Management was outraged. So were the otters. They stuck the muttering crowds and noise for three weeks, waited for the cover of darkness and dug their way out to freedom.

They are reported live and well and living in a nearby forest.

Evolution 2: Firm Management 0

Not deterred, Management then decided as part of the

general improvements to repaint and refurbish the penguin pool. 'It is symbolic of the general slackness' it was said 'that it is so dirty and gloomy. Our public expects better.'

Several gallons of brilliant paint were bought and an artistic effect was achieved at considerable but justifiable cost.

Next day the whole flock of valuable penguins were found with their flippers in the air — not dead, luckily, but temporarily blind. The poor birds were Argentinian penguins and were used to drab grey rocks and ill-adapted to the artificial technicolour tundra.

Evolution 3: Firm Management 0

R. WAGNER'S
PARSI

'SOME OF THE BEST YEAR

...F MY LIFE..' B. LEVIN

BOX OFFICE

Stalls
Royal Circle
Boxes
Away-Day
The Week-ender

COULD I HAVE 4 STALLS, PLEASE, A DOUBLE BED, BATH AND AN EARLY CALL IN THE MORNING?

It doesn't pay to fool with Mother Nature

The balance of ecology is notoriously an area in which decisions have a way of coming back to kick you, generally in an unexpected — and very uncomfortable — way.

For instance, when the family of Master Teddy Hughes emigrated to New South Wales in Australia, he decided to take with him his pet rabbit, 'Cotton Tail' by name, who on arrival proved to be in a delicate condition.

Once in Australia Cotton Tail chose freedom and, untroubled by natural predators, gave birth to her litter in the wild.

As a direct result of Master Hughes's kind heart, a tide of rabbits swept across Australia, until by the 1960s they had become probably the principal animal pest in the Antipodes, costing farmers millions of dollars a year.

Some generations of humans later a French farmer deliberately decided to get even with the rabbits which were plaguing him by introducing a plague of his own, the disease myxomatosis, previously unknown in Europe. (A method similar to that adopted by that enlightened colonist Cecil Rhodes who deliberately spread smallpox among the natives.)

Almost the entire rabbit population of Europe died in

agony before a resistant strain of bunny asserted itself, and then proceeded to multiply far more vigorously than their disease-prone predecessors.

One can only suppose that these stern lessons must have been lost on Dr Warwick Kerr of the University of São Paolo in Brazil. The learned doctor decided that honey production in Brazil needed a boost. The trouble was that Brazilian bees just weren't busy enough. What was required, clearly, was a more energetic and productive bee.

Being a geneticist Dr Kerr was in a position to do something about the situation. He imported twenty-six queen bees from Africa and proceeded to cross them with a docile strain of Italian bee. Unfortunately the resultant bee was of unprecedented ferocity and, furthermore, was armed with a sting which proved lethal to man and animal alike.

When 40,000 of Dr Kerr's bees escaped, panic spread through Brazil as 150 humans and countless animals were stung to death.

All of which would have seemed small beer to Kasipur the Great, King of Anuradnapura, who in approximately 300 AD decided to revolutionalise the agriculture of his country, now Sri Lanka, by the construction of elaborate irrigation works and reservoirs, known as 'tanks'.

His scheme was so successful that he was able to build a city great enough for its renown to reach Rome, whence ambassadors were sent to this powerful but mysterious Eastern potentate.

However, mosquitoes, previously unknown in Ceylon, came to breed on the stagnant waters of his tanks; and the malaria they brought wiped out the entire civilisation in a single generation.

But for self-induced misery all must take second place to a glorious Soviet achievement.

In 1928 First Secretary Joseph Stalin launched a five year plan intended to revolutionise Russian agriculture. Much of the plan was based on the genetic theories of biologist Trofin Denisovitch Lysenko, who believed he could alter crops in a single generation so they would yield far more food. Unfortunately, although a Hero of the Soviet Union, Lysenko was, quite simply, wrong when it came to biology.

His erroneous theories played their part in turning the five year plan into one of the greatest man-made disasters in history. Some ten million people died of starvation. Instead of kicking himself, or indeed Lysenko, Stalin decided to kick his hapless people instead and proceeded to launch a series of great purges in which several million more Russians were liquidated.

A mission
to detain

On August 23rd 1981, a Nigerian businessman, Kizito Idehem, drew £241,000 from his bank in cash, placed it in a black bag and summoned a mini-cab driver, one Kevin Butler, an Irishman from Finsbury Park with a glass eye and a scarred face.

Half way to his destination the businessman decided to go into a shop on an errand, and so asked the mini-cab driver to wait for a few minutes.

Mr Butler drove off at once with the £241,000 and hasn't been seen since.

Investigations are in the reliable hands of Detective Chief Inspector Peter Jay.

Silver with a cloudy lining

Nelson Bunker Hunt and his brother Lamar were, thanks to the family oil business, extremely well-heeled even by Texan standards. But in the autumn of 1979 they embarked on a scheme to get even richer even quicker. With some help from Arab partners, the Hunt brothers set out to corner the entire world supply of silver by purchasing every 'silver future' which came on the market.

Unfortunately for Nelson and Lamar, what they could figure out the US government could figure out too, and given the important role of silver in the world economy, Washington was unenthusiastic about the brothers' little scheme. Just as the Hunts had finished investing ten billion dollars of their own money in the silver market, Uncle Sam changed the rules which covered private investment in precious metals.

The Hunts achieved a record, even if it wasn't the one they had been aiming for. Their personal dealing losses were the largest in history. An unrepentant Nelson was, however, able to dismiss the temporary embarrassment: 'A billion,' he shrugged, 'is not what it used to be.'

Unwise council

In 1978 the London Borough of Camden built a giant new development of prestige flats. For these the architects decided to employ a special type of central heating which warmed the entire three hundred flats by means of ducts implanted in the walls.

Unfortunately, this 'revolutionary' system never functioned properly. In the summer the hapless tenants were unable to turn the heat off — or to open the windows which had been deliberately sealed during the initial construction — so they boiled. In the winter the heating could not be turned up to an acceptable degree, and there was no provision for any other kind of heating, so they froze.

Finally admitting defeat, the Council rehoused those worst affected.

The scheme cost twenty million pounds.

In 1963 the City of Leeds embarked on a £1.25 million scheme to build a giant new swimming pool, not only to provide recreation for the citizens of Leeds, but in order to provide facilities which would enable Leeds to enter into the prestigious and lucrative world of international competitions. Specifically the City Fathers wished to make a bid for the Commonwealth Games.

Accordingly, they decided to engage as architect one

John Poulson from Pontefract, who was not academically qualified as an architect but had many friends.

Opening the baths in 1967 the Lord Mayor, Colonel Lawrence Turnbull, said 'The pool will be a Mecca for the important swimming events of the North'.

Unfortunately, the pool itself was built fractionally too small to comply with international swimming regulations, and so could not be used for serious Olympic standard competition.

Furthermore, the roof became unsafe, the pool itself sprung a leak, and in the end the council claimed £278,000 from the architects for negligence.

OUR ARCHITECT HAS COMPENSATED FOR THIS BAR QUITE BRILLIANTLY WITH A VERY TALL, THIN BAR UPSTAIRS

Down Mexico way

Western 'civilisation' arrived in Mexico in 1517 when a tiny Spanish expedition under stout Cortes landed at Veracruz, intent on the conquest of the fabulously rich New World in the name of the King of Spain.

Montezuma Xocoytzin, Emperor of the Aztecs, a powerful and civilised race, decided that the Spaniards were the reincarnation of the white Aztec God Quetzalcoatl, and forbade his people to resist the conquistadors as they marched on his capital, Tenochtitlan. Thus the Aztec Empire fell, but not before Montezuma had been stoned to death by his own people, incensed by his decision not to fight.

Montezuma set a precedent which was not confined to Mexican history. For example, a century ago there was a considerable fashion for the newer nations to 'borrow' an aristocrat or minor royalty from one of the established European dynasties to lend respectability and tradition to their new constitutions. It was around this period that the Lord Derby was invited to become King of Greece: he declined politely, preferring to remain Earl of Derby.

Another rather surprising character also had the mantle of kingship offered him. During the 1920s a delegation was sent to Great Britain from Albania with instructions to find a wise and powerful king. On their first night in a

London club they fell in with the club bore and asked him who was the most powerful man in the country.

'Lord Northcliffe', he replied, naming the most famous of newspaper magnates.

The delegation duly went to Fleet Street, saw Northcliffe at the *Daily Mail* and offered him their throne. He decided against it, rather as Mr Rupert Murdoch or Sir Robin Day would probably do today if offered the Premiership of, say, Chad.

However, a generation earlier, on April 10th 1863, Archduke Maximillian of Austria did decide to accept the offer of the Imperial Throne of Mexico from Napoleon III of France, who had invaded the country and taken Mexico City.

Unfortunately the idea appealed less to his new subjects than to the French, who obligingly provided him with troops to enforce his rule over the belligerent Mexicans. However, when the United States emerged from its Civil War, it objected strongly to these imperialist goings-on in its own backyard and forced the French to withdraw.

Maximillian was abandoned to his fate and was soon captured by a Mexican liberal army under Generalissimo Juarez. He was executed — dying with great courage and flair — on June 19th 1867.

Suez

Water over the bridge

At midnight on November 3rd 1966, the Italian authorities were awakened and told that the River Arno was about to overflow its banks, and that accordingly the city of Florence should be evacuated forthwith.

The Minister responsible, Signor Taviani, decided to take no action.

Should the populace learn of the danger the roads out of the city would certainly be blocked, the Signor Minister reasoned, by people fleeing in their automobiles. Above all, an order to evacuate would cause panic which was to be avoided at all costs. The Minister returned to bed.

The Arno duly burst its banks.

Somewhat similar circumstances arose in November 1888 when the Committee of the South Fork Fishing and Hunting Club in the Allegheny Mountains decided, yet again, to reject an appeal from the Cambia Iron Company to repair the dam which kept the South Fork Reservoir full up.

The sluice gates must never be opened, they argued, since to do so would disturb both the fish and the tranquillity so valued by the rich members of the Club, many of whom belonged to the best families in Pittsburgh.

On May 31st 1889 freak rain filled the lake to its utmost capacity. At 3.10 p.m. the dam gave way and a wall of water swept into downtown Johnstown.

2,200 people, including many of the Fishing and Hunting Club members, were drowned.

The planned economy

In 1974 the Nigerian Government decided to initiate a 'Third National Nigerian Development Plan', intended to bring the country at a single leap into line with most developed Western nations.

The planners calculated that to build the new roads, airfields and military buildings which the plan required would call for some twenty million tons of cement.

This was duly ordered and shipped by freighters from all over the world, to be unloaded at Lagos Docks.

Unfortunately, the Nigerian planners had not considered the fact that the docks were only capable of handling 2,000 tons a day. Working every day, it would have taken twenty-seven years to unload just the ships which were at one point waiting at sea off Lagos. These contained a third of the world's supply of cement — much of it showing its fine quality by setting solid in the holds of the freighters.

Off
course

In 1910 Bruce Ismay, Chairman of the White Star Line, decided to construct a prestigious new flagship.

It was decided that the mighty liner, which was to draw 46,300 tons, was to follow a novel form of construction with a series of watertight bulkheads running vertically at intervals through her hull.

'We believe the boat is unsinkable', declared the Vice-President of the Line as she set out on her maiden voyage to New York, laden with celebrities and dignitaries. So confident, indeed, were the White Star Line that they neglected to put on board more than a token number of life-boats. The ship was the *Titanic*.

The curse of the ill-fated *Titanic* seems to persist to the present day. In 1979 Lord Grade embarked on his not totally successful epic film, *Raise the Titanic*, at a cost said to be greater than that of the original mighty leviathan of the deep. .

As Lord Grade said ruefully to his shareholders: 'Raise the Titanic . . . . it would have been cheaper to lower the Atlantic.'

AND I'LL TELL YOU
SOMETHING ELSE —
I'M RAPIDLY LOSING
CONFIDENCE IN THIS
LIFE - BELT

In
for a penny

The film business, of course, has always been famous for its decisions, good and bad.

In 1972 a young film director, George Lucas, developed a project for a film to be called *American Graffiti*. The budget was minimal: $700,000. United Artists decided to back it — and then withdrew when the script was completed. Then AIP refused to back it, as it was 'commercially unacceptable'. Universal decided to reject it too — then relented at the last moment.

American Graffiti became one of the highest-grossing pictures of all time.

Fresh from *American Graffiti* Lucas decided that his next project would be a sci-fi movie tentatively titled *Star Wars*. In spite of the success of his first picture nobody seemed to relish the project, not even Universal.

After months a lukewarm Twentieth Century Fox gambled some development money. But Lucas had to raise much of the money himself — all the other established film companies having decided totally against the film.

By the time the film was completed Lucas was flat broke and dispirited — though he, rather than Fox, perforce owned the picture and the rights to any sequels.

In the first four months after its opening in May 1977

Star Wars grossed $134 million. Receipts for the first year exceeded $300 million.

In the year since it opened the sequel, *The Empire Strikes Back*, grossed a further $200 million.

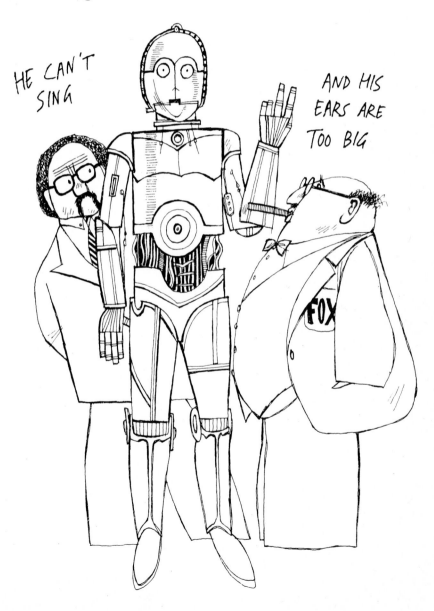

Those wonderful people who brought you The Charge of the Light Brigade

It would be inappropriate here to go into great detail over the prince of bad decisions — the Charge of the Light Brigade. Suffice it to say the General in charge of the Crimea campaign, Lord Raglan, was not on speaking terms with his brother-in-law Lord Lucan who commanded the Light Brigade.

Accordingly when the latter received a loosely-phrased message ordering him to charge the Russian guns he felt unable to inquire *which* guns. He *did* ask the messenger — but the fellow was inconveniently shot dead as he pointed the way.

Mumbling 'Here goes the last of the Brudenells', his Lordship simply rode at the nearest emplacement without bothering to see if he was being followed by his regiment. In the event the Light Brigade did their duty, as did the Cossack gunners, and the British were almost wiped out.

Raglan watched horror-struck from the heights above.

'Don't worry,' said one of his aides-de-camp, trying to console his Commander-in-Chief for the disaster for which he must take responsibility. 'It is nothing compared to the Chillianwalla.'

It is not recorded if Raglan found comfort in these words, but diligent research shows the aide was referring to the Battle of the Chillianwalla in 1849, fought during the Sikh wars.

On this occasion, as was their wont, the turbanned Sikhs cut numerous bits off many poorly led British troops. The corpses, it is said, were disfigured by the Sikhs so that their faces were set into dreadful grins: it was an unprecedented disaster.

Well, perhaps unprecedented is not exactly the right word. From earliest times military decision-making has been unpredictable.

British generalship hardly got off to a flying start. In the year 449 AD King Vortigern of Britain, who was having trouble with the Picts, decided to invite the Saxon brothers Hengist and Horsa to help him in his campaign. The Saxons easily defeated the Picts, but noticing 'the worth-lessness of the Britons and the excellence of the land', sent to Germany for their friends and relations, the Angles and Jutes. They then turned against their erstwhile employer and in 455 AD defeated him at the Battle of Aylesford. Horsa, admittedly, was killed in the fight, but Vortigern's army was defeated and Hengist became the first of the line of Anglo-Saxon kings who ruled Britain for the next six hundred years.

In 1034 AD King Canute decided against all advice to try a stunt which in the event backfired. Another king who had a run-in with the watery deeps was Caligula, in 37 AD. When frustrated in an attempt to cross the Channel and invade Britain he ordered his men into the icy waters to beat the waves with their swords. He then decided to inscribe the defeat of 'Oceana' on his standards. Later the Emperor made his horse consul. History does not relate whether it proceeded to kick him.

From then on the tradition of Imperial disasters continued unabated down the centuries. In January 1842 General Lord Elphinstone, besieged in Kabul by the Afghan Emirs' bloodthirsty troops, decided in spite of much advice as to the untrustworthy nature of the Afghans to accept a safe conduct and withdraw his 16,500 strong garrison ninety miles over the passes to Jalabad.

Elphinstone set out — only to have his entire force massacred as they straggled over the pass. Only one man survived, a Dr Brydon of the Army Medical Corps. This unfortunate, trailing 'arrows and spears like a stuck pig', reached Jalabad where he collapsed. Sir John Kaye the historian wrote: 'It was a tragedy whose awful completeness is unequalled in the history of the world.'

Not surprisingly, given such leadership, things in India went from bad to worse. In 1857 the Governors of the Honourable East India Company issued 223,000 sepoy troops of their army with a new design of Enfield rifle. This required cartridges, made of greased leather, to be bitten through and placed in the breach before firing. Rumours quickly spread that the grease used was a mixture of cow and pig fats. Cows are, of course, sacred to Hindus, and Moslems consider pig meat unclean. Troops of both persuasions thus believed they risked defilement and damnation if they handled their new guns.

On Sunday 10th May 1857, in Meerut, near Delhi,

eighty-five Sepoys of the Second Bengal Grenadiers refused, with expressions of regret and tearful explanations, to obey the order of their British officers to load their new rifles. The Commanding Officer, Major-General W.W. Hewitt repeated the order to load and, when the troops again refused, decided to have his own troops arrested and put in jail.

The same day a group of their comrades, taking rest and recreation in a local brothel, rioted and freed the imprisoned soldiers. Within days the entire East India Company Army had risen and in the ensuing Indian Mutiny untold atrocities were committed on both sides. Tens of thousands died, both Indian and British.

Elsewhere in the British Empire equally perspicacious generals guarded the Imperial flame. On January 22nd 1879 British troops under General the Lord Chelmsford engaged the Zulus under their King Cetewayo at Isandhlwana. So confident were the British of defeating the ignorant, naked savages who opposed them, that they decided it wasn't worth opening in advance the iron-bound wooden boxes in which they kept their ammunition. Furthermore they forgot to bring along any tools capable of opening the chests.

When the ammunition they carried on their persons was exhausted, the British soldiers perforce stopped firing. They were all massacred by the Zulus. Many of the corpses were found with their fingernails torn off in their frantic efforts to claw open the iron boxes.

Bad habits die hard. In the nineteen thirties the Imperial General Staff considered long and hard the problems of defending Britain's Far Eastern Empire and decided to base their strategy upon the island of Singapore. Vast batteries of heavy guns were installed to ensure that the island was impregnable from the sea, and a huge base was constructed to shelter the fleet that would be dispatched thence in time of war.

Little consideration was given to the possibility that Singapore might be threatened from the Malayan mainland, to which it was linked by a causeway. No enemy would come this way, the Generals assured their superiors, for the terrain of Malaya was so rugged as to be totally impenetrable to modern armies. Nor was much urgency attached to air defences, for the admirals considered that aircraft posed little threat to modern ships.

In 1941, the master plan was put into action. The War Cabinet dispatched the two great capital ships, *Prince of Wales* and *Repulse*, to Singapore to overawe the Japanese. To the great surprise of the General Staff, however, the Japanese landed not under the guns of Singapore but on the mainland to the north. *Prince of Wales* and *Repulse* duly sailed to destroy the invasion force and were themselves sunk by a Japanese air attack. The invaders then proceeded to move through the 'impenetrable' terrain of Malaya with astonishing ease and attacked Singapore from the north. The guns being irrevocably pointed out to sea, the city fell within days. 70,000 British and Australian troops surrendered to the Japanese in what Churchill described as 'the largest capitulation in British History'.

'Perfidious Albion' is however as renowned for her brains as for her brawn. Thus, in early 1944, with an Allied victory over Nazi Germany seemingly assured, the British Secret Intelligence Service turned its mind to the possibility that, within the foreseeable future, the Soviet Union would cease to be an ally and become, as it had been in the past, an adversary. With commendable foresight they created a new department, the task of which was to forestall any Soviet espionage directed against Great Britain. The man they chose to head the department was generally considered within the SIS to have a brilliant future.

His name was Harold 'Kim' Philby, and it was indeed the case that he was destined for a top job in intelligence. In 1963, at a press conference in Moscow, he revealed that he held the rank of Colonel in the KGB.

At least MI5 still knew who Kim Philby was — something not to be taken for granted considering a mishap which had overtaken their records in 1940. The then head of the Secret Service, known only by the single letter Q, decided that copies must be made of all records lest the originals be damaged by enemy action. A Secret Service photographer — the records being too sensitive to entrust to outsiders — duly laboured long and hard copying hundreds of documents. It was only when the originals were in fact destroyed by enemy action that it was discovered that in his inexperience and haste the photographer had cropped the top off every negative so the name of the person to whom the file referred was missing.

All in all, perhaps not some of the most glorious pages of British history. But in such matters, too, Britain has no monopoly. Consider this example of good generalship from 'over there'.

On September 17th 1862 the Union and Confederate Armies met at the Battle of Antietam. The Union forces under General Ambrose Burnside were ordered to cross the Potomac River and join battle with their enemies at close quarters.

They decided to cross over the bridge two abreast, presenting an ideal target for the Confederate gunners whose batteries had been specially placed so as to command the bridge. The slaughter was appalling.

General Burnside had failed to discover that the river was only three foot deep and could have been forded on foot at any point with perfect safety.

Of this engagement President Lincoln said: 'Only he could have wrung so spectacular a defeat from the jaws of victory.'

C'est magnifique
but....

For the British, who pride themselves on a monopoly of military disasters, it is salutary to remember that the nation which invented *la gloire* has a record which is not uniformly glorious.

During the early stages of the Battle of Fontenoy, fought in 1745 between the French on the one hand and British and Hanoverian armies on the other, opposing regiments found themselves unexpectedly face to face at the crest of a hill. The British commander, Lord Charles Hill, acted in the best traditions of British sportsmanship and offered the enemy the first shot. '*Messieurs les gardes Français*,' he cried, '*tirez*!' It is not recorded what his troops felt about this sporting offer (very possibly they did not understand French), but they were spared the consequence by the gallantry of the French commander who, refusing to be outdone in courtesy, replied, doffing his hat '*Messieurs les Anglais, tirez le premier.*'* The British volley which followed decimated the French formation and led to a British victory in the battle.

* Some French scholars insist that the correct punctuation is: '*Messieurs! Les Anglais! Tirez le premier!*'

On September 1st, 1870, a French army led by the Emperor Napoleon III in person chose to encamp at Sedan, on the eve of the first major engagement in a war against Prussia provoked by the French Emperor in search of *la gloire*, and of some distraction for his people. Unfortunately the Emperor was too sick even to sit on his horse, and furthermore, unlike his famous uncle, he had no experience whatsoever of war.

One old French Marshal remarked on seeing the battlefield selected by his Emperor: '*Nous sommes dans la pot de chambre et nous y seront enmerder!*' — We are all in the chamber pot and will be shat on!

In the event, he was proved resoundingly right. 20,000 French soldiers were killed and 80,000 taken prisoner. Napoleon III himself surrendered to the Kaiser. On September 4th the Second Empire fell and a Third Republic was established in France.

One of the factors leading to the catastrophic defeat of the French at the battle of Sedan was the superiority of the Prussians' steel guns, manufactured by Alfred Krupp, over the older, bronze guns used by the French. Indeed, the effectiveness of these weapons seemed to symbolise the aggression of the new German State and the prosperity of the Ruhr steel masters who armed it. What is less generally known is that Herr Krupp had gone to great lengths, before the war, to persuade the French High Command of the merits of his new weapons and the benefits which they would gain by buying them. His correspondence was filed by French Staff Officers in a folder labelled 'Rien à faire' — 'no action required'.

Nor was the Great War better for la gloire. In 1914 a party of French soldiers were demonstrating their Imperial presence by sailing an armoured tug-boat up and down the Congo river near Ouesso. However, come the heat of the noon, they disembarked intending to take a siesta. As they picnicked on the river bank their African sailors came running to warn them that a German gunboat was on its way down river from the Cameroons and was about to pounce on them.

The French, flush with good wine and food, decided not

to move. Exclamations of *'Je m'en fous! Je m'en fous!'* — 'I don't give a damn!' were heard to ring through the bush.

Their native sailors fled. The Germans landed, crept up through the jungle and slew the entire French contingent. A monument, called locally *'le monument de je m'en fous'* stands to this day on the river bank.

In May 1953 the French commander in Indo China, General Henri Navarre, frustrated by the refusal of his Viet Minh opponents to stand and fight the kind of set-piece battle for which his troops were trained and equipped, decided to lure the enemy into a trap.

In November of that year his plans went into effect and 16,500 crack French paratroops were dropped into an impenetrable wooded valley called Dien Bien Phu, deep behind the enemy lines. Navarre reasoned that the Viet Minh would find the bait irresistible and would devote all their resources to an attempt to overrun the French bridgehead. The French force could be supplied by air, but Navarre's experts reckoned that the Viet Minh would find it impossible to bring up heavy guns and supplies through the jungles which surrounded the landing site, so they would inevitably be crushed by the might of French arms.

Alas, it was Navarre's misfortune to be opposed by General Giap, generally reckoned to be one of the greatest military geniuses ever. Giap mobilised 50,000 coolies, who carried heavy guns, dismantled into their component pieces, through the jungle into commanding positions overlooking the French force. When the coming of the rainy season made air supply and support virtually impossible, Giap literally pounded Navarre's force into the

111

mud. After suffering terrible casualties the French surrendered. It was the end of French colonialism in Indo China, and the beginning of another famously bad decision — America's involvement in Vietnam.

In the course of the many and various bad decisions of 'Nam' the following little-known example deserves a footnote.

In the late 1960s some officers in the US Air Force determined that the Thanh Hoa bridge, some ninety miles south of Hanoi, was a 'key bottleneck' in the North Vietnamese supply system and therefore a prime target in the bombing campaign which President Johnson had unleashed on that country. Over the next few years, according to North Vietnamese claims, one hundred US aircraft were shot down over Thanh Hoa without any substantial damage being caused to the bridge. Finally, in May 1972, the bridge was demolished by one of the new 'smart bombs'.

This hard-won success did not greatly inconvenience the Vietnamese, who had been using a ford five miles downstream for years. But the Thanh Hoa bridge had not been without value to them. As a US officer pointed out wryly, 'They had a flourishing anti-aircraft school at one end'.

Bourbons
on the rocks

Given the remarkable talent which most of its kings have displayed for getting things wrong, the wisest thing France ever did was to become a Republic — or rather, a sequence of Republics.

On 26th August 1346 Philip VI of France confronted an English army led by Edward the Black Prince at Crécy in the Somme Valley. In the course of the battle Philip saw that his forces were retreating. Outraged at this cowardice, and carried away in the heat of the moment, he ordered the rest of his army to attack their erstwhile comrades as well as the English.

Not surprisingly, Crécy was something of a disaster for the French. 1,500 French noblemen were slain by the English or by each other; losses in the English ranks totalled just fifty dead.

After another four and a half centuries of this sort of leadership, the French people decided to dispense with royalty. The methods they adopted were extreme and in the winter of 1792 their last King, Louis XVI, fled from the terror in Paris. He paused at Vincennes to take refreshments and, having finished his meal, offered the innkeeper a golden 'Louis' in payment — the contemporary

YOU ARE LOUIS XVI
AND I CLAIM
MY FIVE POUNDS

equivalent of trying to pay for a beer and a sandwich with a £50 note. The innkeeper was moved to take a second look at this startlingly affluent customer and at once recognised the King from his likeness on the coin which bore his name. Louis was seized and taken back to Paris where, in January 1793, he and his family were executed.

Even when they got a chance of regaining their throne, French royalty managed to blow it.

In October 1872, in the wake of France's disastrous defeat at the hands of the Prussians, the Government's republican ardour faltered and it offered the crown to Henri Charles Ferdinand, Comte de Chambord, who preferred to be known as King Henri V. Maréchal MacMahon, Duke of Magenta, announced the good news to the future king with the words, '*L'heure est arrivé!*' But Henri refused to seize *l'heure*; the Government would first, he declared, have to abolish the hateful republican tricolour and return to the white flag of the Bourbons. When the Maréchal explained that to promise this would exceed his authority, the Comte replied 'You will be back'. And stepped forever from the stage of history.

Escargot malvenu

In July 1979 Marc Quinquandon of France, intent on bringing home his share of *la gloire*, attempted the world snail-eating record. The intrepid Frenchman managed to consume 144 snails in eleven minutes and thirty seconds. A lesser man might have been satisfied with this achievement, but M. Quinquandon knew that he had it in him to set an unbeatable record for all time.

Four months later, after undergoing a rigorous training, he consumed seventy-two snails in a mere three minutes.

His record, however, proved to be posthumous. Marc Quinquandon died in his hour of triumph — of snail poisoning.

ALAS, HE FORGOT TO SPIT OUT ZE SHELLS

The law is an ass

As befits the man who gave his name to the rules of boxing, the 8th Marquis of Queensberry was no admirer of literature nor of unmanly behaviour. In particular he was infuriated by the friendship between Oscar Wilde and his son Lord Alfred Douglas, known to Wilde as 'Bosie'.

In May 1895 the Marquis called at Wilde's club and left his card inscribed with the words: 'To Oscar Wilde, posing as a somdomite'. (The Marquis was evidently no great speller.)

Egged on by Bosie, Wilde decided to sue the Marquis for libel. But the case collapsed in court, and Wilde was prosecuted and sentenced to two years imprisonment for sodomy. On his release from Reading Jail he went into exile for the rest of his life.

That, perhaps, is a good example of the dangers of 'going to law'. It is not for nothing that when a lawyer represents himself in court the rest of the fraternity describe him as 'having a fool as a client'.

Consider also the graphic fate of Ms St Claire who tried to stick up for her rights by means of litigation. In December 1980 Ms Lindi St Claire, a London prostitute who specialised in providing 'discipline' and other exotic recreation for her clients, decided it would be advantageous to register her highly lucrative enterprise as a company. The Registrar of Companies was willing to accept a definition of the business as providing 'personal services',

but refused to sully his register with the franker 'hooker', 'prostitute', or even 'French-lessons teacher'. Affronted by such official prudery, Ms St Claire took the Registrar to court, where, in a widely reported case, Lord Justice Ackner found against her.

Alas for Ms St Claire; the readership of the law reports was not limited to prospective clients or even students of company law. On 17th February 1981 Inspectors from the Inland Revenue called on her at Eardley Crescent, West London and, having inspected her business premises, which included a well-equipped dungeon, delivered their own form of 'discipline': an assessment of income tax liability totalling £10,768 75p.

There's none so blind...

On April 13th 1977, Miss Yvonne Whittlesham, also known as 'The Psychic Escapologist', decided to celebrate the Queen's Silver Jubilee with a 60 mph 'Blindfold Dash'.

Accordingly, she donned an iron blindfold and set off in a powerful car, her foot hard on the accelerator.

She crashed headlong into the side of a barn within four hundred yards, a mere 59¾ miles short of her target.

They said it would never work

In the late nineteenth century America was invention-mad. Men such as Thomas Edison and Alexander Graham Bell showed that inventors and their financial backers could grow rich on ingenuity and science. The only problem was choosing the right inventor. In 1874 a group of Wall Street speculators was convinced that a certain John Worrell Keely had come up with an idea which, at the asking price of $1 million, just had to be a snip.

Mr Keely demonstrated to the would-be entrepreneurs the powers of his discoveries, 'vibratory energy', 'etheric vapour' and 'inter-atomic ether'. If the performance of his wonderful, fully operational laboratory models was anything to go by, 'vibratory energy', when fully exploited, would perform miracles such as propelling cannon balls through walls, or enabling an engine to run at 800 revolutions per minute for fifteen days fuelled by a thimbleful of water, or even crossing the Atlantic on a pint of water. People queued up to invest in these miracles of science and technology.

In 1898, having pocketed his million dollars, Mr Keely expired from over-indulgence. His backers were naturally hopeful that something could be salvaged from the wreck and eagerly ransacked his laboratory in the hope that its secrets would be revealed. They were — in the form of a tank of compressed air beneath the floor which fed his demonstration models through concealed brass tubes. The million dollars was a write off.

If Keely's backers were too gullible, then the Remington Arms Company was over-cautious. In 1897 the firm was offered the rights to a patent writing machine owned by the Wagner Typewriting Machine Co. Remington decided, literally, to stick to their guns, explaining that it was their belief that 'no mere machine can replace a reliable and honest clerk'.

In due course the Wagner enterprise was taken over by the Underwood Company who, over the following fifty years, managed to sell more than twelve million of the 'mere machines'.

Nor were poor commercial decisions confined to the United States. At the turn of the last century the silk mills of Lister & Co in Bradford were the most prosperous in the United Kingdom. Their owners had built them accordingly — a coach and four could be driven round the top of the chimney of the Lister works.

In 1912 a chemist and scientist called on Listers to offer them a new invention: his name was Samuel Courtauld, and the discovery he offered was a synthetic silk called 'rayon'.

Listers turned him away indignantly. 'It will never catch on — the public will never accept artificial silks. Listers will stay with the *real* thing.'

Which they did.

Samuel Courtauld, however, set up for himself and waxed exceeding rich.

123

Another sadder but wiser inventor who failed to become rich from his brainwave was Arthur C. Clarke, the sci-fi author. In 1945 he invented the communications satellite, published its specification in *Wireless World* and turned his hand to fiction.

'Comsat', which owns and operates the fruits of his foresight, is one of the world's largest corporations. As a consolation prize it gave Arthur Clarke ten shares — total dividend income 17 cents.

But if the sage of Sri Lanka gets to brooding in his palatial house in Colombo, he may find comfort in hearing a *real* reason to kick oneself.

The tale is told of Lana Turner's grandfather who owned a half share in a small firm which made a soft drink called Coca-Cola. Despairing of a product burdened with so unappealing a name, he sold out. He had not, however, lost faith in the soft drinks business, so he invested the proceeds in a firm he deemed more likely to flourish — the Raspberry Cola Company.

A few years later the Coca-Cola Company, which in the meantime had done rather better than its one-time co-owner had anticipated, was offered the twice-bankrupt Pepsi-Cola Company. Its then owner, Charles Guth of Loft Inc, was willing to let his subsidiary go for a mere $1000. But with an over-confidence born of their virtual monopoly of the soft drink business, Coca-Cola spurned the offer, thus missing the opportunity to strangle at birth the business which would in due course become their arch rival.

Cuckoo clock

On April 26th, 1981, Conservative MP Richard Alexander called in the Bomb Squad to deal with an ominously ticking parcel which had been delivered to his constituency office in Retford, Nottinghamshire.

An X-Ray revealed a timing mechanism and the squad therefore duly decided to blow up the parcel.

The debris turned out to consist of the MP's spare pyjamas, toothbrush, razor and a travelling clock, the gift of his wife. They had been forwarded to him by a hotel where he had left them after a speaking engagement.

Porridge

In the autumn of 1980 the Governor of Featherstone Prison, near Northampton, decided to allow the prisoners to embark on an ambitious and therapeutic programme of pottery-making in the prison workshops.

So adept did some of the inmates become that their output, which they were allowed to purchase back for the cost of the clay, 30p a piece, became an object of admiration throughout the Prison Service. On one occasion the Governor himself watched a batch going through the kiln.

However, unbeknownst to him, the inmates were using the facilities to produce nigh-perfect copies of the work of the famous potter Bernard Leach, including forged signatures and stamps, as well as the distinctive glazes characteristic of the master.

The pieces were then smuggled out of the prison and sold for high prices in Sotheby's, Christie's and Bonhams, one piece going for over £1,000. Suspicions arose only when the market became flooded with 'new' Leach masterpieces.

The manufacture of masterpieces, artistic and literary, has always had an irresistible attraction for the criminal — and often for the intended victim.

Perhaps the most famous forger of recent times was the Dutchman Hans van Meegeren who, rebuffed in his attempts to become a serious painter, turned his hand to running up Vermeers.

He invented a whole new period and style of the 16th century master's works and claimed to have found an old attic stuffed full of dusty canvasses.

Critics hailed them as undoubted masterpieces — and van Meegeren sold them gleefully for enormous sums, often to the Nazi occupying forces.

On July 12th 1945 he was arrested and charged with treasonously selling off national art treasures. In a desperate state, he decided to admit that the paintings were all forgeries, figuring it was better to be done as a forger than as a traitor.

Nobody believed him.

Even more desperately, he sent for paints and canvass and ran up a 'Vermeer' in the court. Only then did he achieve his conviction for forgery, and depart gratefully for prison.

On the literary front, in 1972 McGraw Hill paid one Clifford Irving $75,000 for millionaire recluse Howard Hughes's 'autobiography'. They proclaimed that they were 'totally satisfied' of its authenticity. Howard Hughes himself emerged to hold a telephonic press conference at which he denounced the book as a fake. McGraw Hill stuck to their guns. Finally Irving confessed that the whole thing *was* a fake. He went to jail — the publishers lost their money.

And so did the *Sunday Times* when in 1967 it purchased 'Mussolini's diaries' for £250,000. In exchange for an E type Jaguar and £30,000 the Duce's son, 'Boots' Mussolini, a jazz pianist, agreed to authenticate them.

Unfortunately the documents had been forged in Northern Italy by a little old lady, a Mrs Amalia, who had sold them to a friend, Mrs Panvini-Rosati, who made a living selling such things for modest sums. They had already been convicted for forgery and now labelled their concoctions 'historical curiosities'. Their story was well known in Italian scholarly circles.

Unfortunately the *Sunday Times* had decided to negotiate the price of its major scoop in the utmost secrecy — which precluded consulting their Rome correspondent or even their own cuttings library, which could have turned up the story of the two ingenious Italian ladies within minutes.

Face the music

The definitive musical mistake of all time was made in 1962 by Dick Rowe, an 'Artist and Repertory' man employed by Decca. In March of that year Mr Rowe had a visit from a Liverpool piano shop owner, Brian Epstein, who had just undertaken to manage an unknown pop group and wanted Rowe to hear their demonstration record.

After listening to the disc, Rowe told his visitor that he did not want to take the group on. 'I am sorry, Brian,' he is reported to have said, 'groups with guitars are on their way out.'

Brian Epstein, however, persevered and finally got a contract for his group from George Martin of EMI. Within six years the Beatles had sold 100 million albums and 100 million singles including 'I want to hold your hand', the best selling British single of all time, with global sales of 13 million. Guitars were on their way in again.

Twenty years later, in August 1981, a politically minded pop group from Woolwich decided to hold a concert to protest against the National Front's exploitation of punk music to popularise its racial policies. They called their concert satirically 'A Rock Against Ginger-Haired People'. It was well attended and their joke was much appreciated by their sophisticated audience.

Next day the leader of the group was on his way to his next gig when a car drew up and four ginger-haired people leaped out and beat him over the head with a lump of wood until he was insensible.

ROCK AGAINST BEARDS

That satirical pop group was heir to a long and noble tradition in popular music by which black and white musicians work and play freely together. They have not done so, however, without having to face great difficulties — especially in the deep South — and the results could be tragic.

At 10.00 p.m. on September 26th 1937 Dr Hugh Smith, a surgeon from Memphis, came to the scene of a traffic accident on Route 61, ten miles north of Clarkesdale, Mississippi. There were two victims. One, a white man, was slightly concussed and Dr Smith sent him to a nearby hospital, where he recovered. The other victim was a black woman who was far more severely injured. Dr Smith decided that, rather than being sent to Clarkesdale like her white manager, Bessie Smith, the greatest Blues singer ever to draw breath, should be sent to a distant 'blacks only' hospital. She bled to death during the journey.

The classical equivalent of turning down the Beatles must be firing Mozart, and that is exactly what Archbishop Count Hieronymus von Colloredo did on April 3rd 1780. After the production of Mozart's first great opera, *Idomeneo*, in Munich, the Archbishop dismissed him from his post as court composer on the grounds of incompetence and, two months later, had him kicked out of the palace gates by a lackey.

Composers also seem to put their foot — or in one case, fingers — in it.

On June 14th, 1832, musical prodigy and potential virtuoso Robert Schumann invented a 'finger tormentor', a gadget designed to take some of the tedious strain out of practising on the piano. The machine raised the forefinger automatically and allowed extra training for the other digits.

Within a few months the machine had so damaged Schumann's fingers that he never played the piano again.

Nor is it only managers, patrons or luckless composers who, in the eyes of history, make fools of themselves. In 1844 the London Philharmonic Orchestra was rehearsing for the first British performance of Franz Schubert's 'Great C Major' Symphony. Felix Mendelssohn was conducting the work as an act of homage, but in spite of Mendelssohn's enthusiasm for the composition, the orchestra had its own opinion.

'Hey, Tom!' the horn player called to a colleague in mid-rehearsal, 'have you been able to discover a tune yet?' No one had, and to Mendelssohn's anguish, the entire orchestra downed instruments and walked out.

Head over heels

On June 7th, 1977, Philip Dubois, honeymooning on the romantic island of Réunion, returned from a midnight stroll.

He decided, in a flush of nuptial enthusiasm, to vault over the fence surrounding his hired honeymoon cottage and surprise and delight Mrs Dubois.

Unfortunately Mr Dubois had mistaken his way in the darkness. He plunged headlong into the crater of the Ganga volcano, and died.

Always a mistake

INVADING RUSSIA

MARRYING HENRY VIII

ACCEPTING A CABINET POST IN IRAQ OR
LIBERIA

. . . .

All at sea

In the autumn of 1904, after the Russian forces in the Far East had been severely defeated by the Japanese, Czar Nicholas II was persuaded that the only chance of redressing the balance lay in dispatching his Baltic Fleet halfway around the world to teach the Japanese a lesson. The fleet duly set out from Riga under the Imperial Admiral, Prince Rozhestrensky.

Two days later the Prince was summoned from his bunk in the middle of the night with the news that his ships were about to come under fire from enemy vessels. The Prince felt there was no time to be lost. Without pausing to consider the real likelihood that the Imperial Japanese Navy would have come to fight a decisive battle off the Dogger Bank, he ordered his ironclads to open fire.

The Russian gunners jumped to it, and to considerable effect: they hit and sank no less than sixty-three vessels. Unfortunately these turned out to be forty-eight steam-trawlers, three mother ships and twelve trawlers owned by Messrs Layman & Co, all members of the Hull fishing fleet, peacefully fishing for cod. The casualties among their crews consisted of two seamen drowned and six wounded by shellfire.

Prince Rozhestrensky, however, did not pause to make a tally of the devastation he had inflicted upon the fishermen, but steamed on at full speed for the Sea of Japan. There, five months later, his fleet encountered a

136

more formidable adversary. On 27th May 1905 the Japanese fleet sallied forth from its concealed anchorage behind the island of Tsu-Shima and totally destroyed the Prince's ships in a matter of hours.

The Russians, of course, have no great seafaring tradition and such mishaps could never befall a service with a record like the Royal Navy .... Or could they?

Consider the case of grizzled seadog Sir Cloudesley Shovell, who found himself in 1704 returning to port in Cornwall, carrying a priceless treasure of Greek antiques from Naples, the property of Emma Hamilton's husband, Sir William Hamilton.

Off the Scillies he had a violent quarrel with his pilot, and decided to hang him on the yard-arm for insubordination. He promptly lost his way, ran aground on the underwater rocks and sank. Ship, sailors and treasure went to the bottom.

There being something of a closed season in maritime adventures in 1910, Captain Robert Falcon Scott RN sailed for the Antarctic on board the *Terra Nova*, intent on reaching the North Pole on foot. Previous explorers advised him emphatically that his sledges must be pulled by dogs, but he decided that ponies would be better. When the animals could go no further, he said, the intrepid explorers would pull the loads themselves.

This method of travel proved hopelessly ill-adapted for the ordeal. By the end of March 1912 all members of Scott's expedition, men and animals, had perished in the arctic wastes.

A specially striking triumph of British naval planning came in 1917, at the height of the Great War, when the British Admiralty decided to construct a flotilla of K-boats — giant 325-foot-long steam-powered submarines.

K2 caught fire on its first dive.
K3 sank to the bottom with the Prince of Wales on board and had to be salvaged.
K3 was then rammed by K6 on manoeuvres and sank.
K4 ran aground.
K5 sank with loss of all hands.
K7 rammed K17 and had to be scrapped.
K14 sprung a leak while still in dock.
Later, at sea, K14 rammed K22 and sank.
K17, during the same sea trials, rammed first an escorting cruiser and then K7. K17 then went out of control and sank.
K22 was rammed by another escorting cruiser.

In 1918 the K-boat project was abandoned. 250 British sailors had been killed.

If British naval history inspired Mr Prasantha Mukherjee, when in 1977 he decided to save on air fares and sail home to Calcutta, then it must have been the example of the bemused commanders of the K-boats rather than that of Drake or Nelson.

Undaunted by his total lack of sailing experience, Mr Mukherjee bought a yacht, the *Chintra*, and provisioned her for the long voyage with lentils, curry powder and Quaker Oats.

Ten miles out from the Hamble, he ran aground and had

to be saved by a combined Anglo-French naval rescue team. The cost to the taxpayer was in excess of £80,000.

But such a sum was mere chicken feed — or perhaps fish meal — compared with the damage done by an earlier sea dog. In 1893 a British battle fleet under Vice-Admiral Sir George Tryon was engaged on sea manoeuvres off Tripoli. The Admiral, on the bridge of his flagship HMS *Victoria*, decided to order his ship to turn to port.

Realising that this would put the flagship on a collision course with HMS *Camperdown*, and that the Admiral had confused port and starboard, his Flag Captain, Maurice Brook, queried the order.

'Do as I say,' bellowed the Admiral, 'Or I'll have you court-martialled.'

His officers accordingly stood stoically to attention on the bridge as HMS *Victoria* and HMS *Camperdown* collided and sank.

Sir George went down with his ship.

I AM NOT GOING DOWN WITH MY SHIP, SIR, I AM GOING DOWN WITH YOUR BLOODY SHIP

Epilogue

I met a traveller from an antique land
Who said: Two vast and trunkless legs of stone
Stand in the desert. Near them, on the sand,
Half sunk, a shattered visage lies, whose frown
And wrinkled lip, and sneer of cold command,
Tell that its sculptor well those passions read
Which yet survive (stamped on these lifeless things),
The hand that mocked them and the heart that fed;
And on the pedestal these words appear:
'My name is Ozymandias, king of kings,
Look on my works, ye Mighty, and despair.'
Nothing beside remains. Round the decay
Of that colossal wreck, boundless and bare,
The lone and level sands stretch far away.

Percy Bysshe Shelley

P.S. AN INVITATION

Undeterred by the signal failure of their earlier attempts at the solicitation of material, described on p. 14, and emboldened by the inherent good taste (or at least staying power) that the reader has demonstrated by getting as far as this, the compilers have decided to try again.

They would like to invite readers to submit contributions, or remedy what they regard as grievous omissions, for the second volume of *I Could Have Kicked Myself*, subject, of course, to Mr André Deutsch making the good/bad/indifferent* decision that there should be such a volume.

All successful contributors will be acknowledged, and the prizes for winning entries will include a copy of the Complete Works of Selma Ottiliana Lovisa Lagerlof, a private screening of *Raise the Titanic*, a luxury cruise for two aboard the *Chintra* under the personal supervision of Mr Mukherjee, and a blindfold dash around the edge of the Ganga volcano with the psychic escapologist herself at the wheel.

R.S.V.P.
David Frost & Michael Deakin
c/o André Deutsch
105 Great Russell Street
London WC1B 3LJ

* delete that which is inapplicable